THE HUSTLE
A KOREAN FAMILY'S ESCAPE FROM THE MARGINS
THREE GENERATIONS OF WORK AND RESILIENCE
KANG EUNJIN

The Hustle : A Korean Family's Escape from the Margins

"This is a story about the lives of workers—our own lives, our families, and our neighbors—that we all thought we knew, yet no one truly spoke about. Without diving into controversial issues or grand social debates, the book presents these stories through the lens of the author's family members, offering us a clear and honest reflection—like looking into a mirror."

"Even if you're not particularly interested in labor or social issues, I

recommend this book as a moment to pause, reflect, and offer comfort to the lives of your own family or neighbors— much like checking in with yourself when you look in the mirror."

"The stories of the protagonists, who work tirelessly as members of society yet cannot escape poverty, feel deeply personal—like the stories of my own family and friends. It made me realize that poverty is not just an individual problem."

"Despite not having dramatic twists or novel elements, the book never felt boring. It is a concise retelling of a family's life story, based on true events. The narrative weaves in the lives of three generations—three daughters of the author's parents' generation and their children—while subtly intertwining modern and contemporary Korean history."

"By objectively analyzing poverty and hard labor, which reflect both the

author's family and my own, I found comfort in realizing that these struggles aren't caused by laziness or personal failings."

"At first, I thought the topic might be heavy, but I found myself reading quickly because the writing flows so smoothly. What stood out most is that it's not a hard, academic read—it's a relatable story about people we know, people like our families."

"The author presents their family's labor history with an objective yet gentle touch, yet throughout, I felt the warmth and care of an artist. This made the reading experience deeply emotional."

Prologue

Whenever I heard the words, "They're someone's family, too. Please refrain from verbal abuse and swearing," I couldn't help but think, "They're not just 'someone'—they're *my* family." This realization struck deeply, especially when I considered that my loved ones might face such mistreatment in their workplaces.

Motorcycle courier, janitor, call center operator, restaurant server, grocery store staff, food delivery worker—these are the jobs my mom, dad, sisters, and nephews do.

Media often depicts scenes where uniformed students encounter their parents working these jobs and react with embarrassment, ashamed of their family's occupations. Seeing such portrayals made me wonder how I would respond in a similar situation. Rather than answering, I found myself simply hoping never to face it.

I am a white-collar office worker. I wear an employee ID around my neck and sit at a desk. I've been working for 15 years—long enough to be considered experienced, even old. Yet, I still feel uneasy at the thought of encountering my family members at my workplace.

What if my dad arrives at my office building, delivering packages on his motorcycle? What if I run into my sister serving at a restaurant during a business meal? Or my nephew dropping off food at my workplace? Or my mom cleaning the very office where I work?

I love and respect my family. I know the dignity of their honest labor. Yet, the thought of these moments fills me with an unshakable apprehension. And that unease—more than anything else—disappoints me.

This book is a reflection on my family's labor and a personal confession.

Is Labor a Punishment?

Unlike me, working in an air-conditioned office, my family endures the harsh elements—braving snow, rain, and the scorching sun. While I am met with consistent professional courtesy and respectful treatment, my family faces challenges, often encountering disrespect, verbal aggression, and hostility in their workplaces.

Even within my comfortable professional setting, I carry a deep sense of guilt over these disparities.

The easiest way to shield myself from this guilt is to turn away—to ignore the weight of their struggles. It feels easier not to know how exhausting their work is or how unfairly they are treated. I tell myself that I can't change their circumstances, that my own survival in the professional world demands my full attention.

My dad, during his years as a motorcycle courier, would describe his job as merely "picking up coins scattered on the street." My nephew Jihoon, despite working twelve-hour shifts six days a week, insists, "It's not that hard—just a lot of standing." My other nephew, Minjoon, lost patches of hair from stress at his part-time job, yet dismisses any concern with a smile. My mom, even before collapsing from exhaustion while performing janitorial duties, only ever shared the good moments—small gestures of kindness from office workers who left her thank-you notes or cups of coffee.

They never told me how hard it was. And I chose to believe them.

Another way to ease my guilt was to shift the blame onto them. If I convinced myself that my family's hardships were the result of their own shortcomings—lack of ability, insufficient motivation, inadequate effort, or even excessive material desires—I could justify their struggles as consequences of their own failings.

But that wasn't true.

My dad worked as a motorcycle courier for over two decades, braving snow and rain without fail, starting when I was in high school. His earnings paid for my university tuition and living expenses, allowing me to study without financial worry. My sister Jiyoung balanced preparing for the college entrance exams with part-time jobs, all while supporting my studies and making sure I had meals every day. My sister Yoojung would return from restaurant shifts on winter nights with swollen hands from washing dishes in freezing water, yet she still managed to clean the house and cook dinner.

To avoid facing the truth—that I had benefited from their sacrifices—I tried to convince myself that their struggles were their own doing. If I could believe that, I wouldn't have to acknowledge how much I owed them. Their hard work had to be a *punishment*—a consequence of ignorance, incompetence, or arrogance.

In the end, this manifested as resentment toward my family.

To me, they became like invisible figures—always present, yet unseen.

Labor History of Three Generations

Based on my family's experiences and interviews with my dad, two older sisters, and two nephews, I compiled our labor history. These interviews took place over one to three sessions per person, each lasting about two hours, between August 2021 and January 2022. Family members without work experience were not included. The ages listed are as of 2022, and all names, except for mine, are pseudonyms.

For the purpose of this history, *labor* is defined as "earning money outside the home," meaning housework and caregiving within the family are not included.

Chapter 1: Youngsoo Kang

From Factory Owner to Courier Driver: The Rise and Fall of a Self-Made Entrepreneur

Born in 1949, in the poverty-stricken aftermath of the Korean War, my dad grew up with little. Yet through sheer determination and relentless hard work, he climbed from being a factory worker in a small bag manufacturing plant to owning his own factory—embodying the South Korean dream during the economic boom of the 1960s and 70s. His entrepreneurial drive pushed him further, expanding his business into the wholesale distribution of bag materials. At the peak of his success, our family enjoyed the comforts of a 1,500-square-foot apartment in Seoul and owned two cars—symbols of his achievements.

Then came the devastating IMF crisis of 1997, which brought my dad's thriving business empire to its knees. Forced to start over, he turned to work as a motorcycle courier. Unlike his earlier years, when perseverance alone could overcome hardship, the new economic reality was unyielding, no matter how hard he worked. For two decades, he made a living on his motorcycle, navigating the city through rain, snow, and traffic. And when the COVID-19 pandemic struck in 2020, it brought his working life to an end, leaving his dream of starting his own courier service unfulfilled.

Chapter 2: Jiyoung Kang

From Part-Time Hustles to Corporate Stability: A Fight for a Career

My second-oldest sister, Jiyoung (born 1977), was preparing for her second college entrance exam when our family's financial foundation collapsed. As she pursued her dream of becoming a teacher, she juggled her studies with a grueling series of part-time jobs—working at convenience stores, cafes, restaurants, and department stores. But despite her efforts, she was unable to gain admission to college.

After several failed attempts to enter university, Jiyoung shifted her focus to finding work. But this was during South Korea's most challenging post-IMF unemployment crisis, making job opportunities scarce. She continued to patch together part-time jobs while also attending vocational training. Her persistence paid off in 2000 when she secured a position as a telephone operator at KT, a public corporation, though initially on a contract basis.

In the aftermath of the IMF crisis, KT underwent privatization and restructuring, which briefly created opportunities for contract workers to transition into permanent roles. Jiyoung seized this opportunity, and her career trajectory shifted from part-time worker to contract employee, eventually becoming a permanent corporate staff member. As her job stability grew, so did her quality of life. Later, Jiyoung got married and chose to leave the workforce, embracing her current role as a full-time homemaker.

Chapter 3: Yoojung Kang

A Single Mother's Journey: From Struggle to Independence

My oldest sister, Yoojung (born 1975), began her career as a bookkeeper at a major pharmaceutical company after graduating from vocational high school. However, she left her job upon marriage. At 29, she found herself a single mother, solely responsible for her two young children, aged 3 and 5. To support them, Yoojung took whatever work she could find—dishwashing, kitchen assistance, and cashiering at a supermarket. While it allowed her to manage her childcare duties, the work offered little financial security, making it impossible to survive independently without our family's support.

When her children entered middle and high school, Yoojung gained more flexibility in her schedule and began working as a truck courier. Her earnings depended on her effort and ability rather than being constrained by the minimum wage. This shift finally allowed her to achieve financial independence and support her children without relying on family assistance. Today, Yoojung continues to work as a truck courier, and her children are now adults.

Chapter 4: Minjoon Lee

The Struggles of Student Workers: Balancing Education and Employment

My nephew Minjoon (born 2001) entered the workforce at just sixteen, accumulating six years of labor experience by the time he turned twenty-two. His introduction to work began in middle school with grueling twelve-hour shifts at a restaurant. By high school, he was delivering food until 5 AM, enduring relentless exploitation—days off were so rare they could be counted on one hand. Struggling to balance his education, he became chronically late for school. Yet, despite being both a student and a worker, he was protected as neither.

Even after enrolling in college, Minjoon continued working part-time. However, his job at a hotel exposed him to a different labor environment. For the first time, he experienced legal employment protections—insurance, benefits, scheduled holidays, and overtime pay. Unlike his previous exploitative jobs, this workplace provided structured professional development and a clear path for advancement: from part-time to intern, from intern to full-time employee. While working at the hotel, Minjoon saw firsthand how language skills could open doors to better career opportunities. Now serving his mandatory military duty, he dedicates his free time to studying English, determined to secure a more promising future upon returning to civilian life.

Chapter 5: Jihoon Lee

Around and Around: The Motorcycle Delivery Circuit

My nephew Jihoon (born 1999) "earned" his first 1 million won through illegal online gambling at just thirteen years old, during his first year of middle school. This early exposure warped his perception of money and labor—gambling wasn't a reckless vice but an alternative source of income. Whenever life became unstable—whether after running away from home or losing a job—he turned back to gambling, only to sink deeper into debt. As a high school freshman, burdened by mounting gambling debts, Jihoon made the life-altering decision to drop out of school. To make ends meet, he took up motorcycle food delivery—a job that was dangerous and physically demanding, but one that promised quick money.

At twenty, Jihoon sought stability by taking jobs frying chicken at a restaurant and managing a café. But without an academic background, specialized skills, or experience, he had little choice but to take on physically demanding, dangerous, or exhausting work. The relentless nature of these jobs led him to quit frequently, leaving him financially unstable. Desperation pushed him back to gambling, hoping to recover his losses. Today, Jihoon remains a motorcycle food delivery driver, caught in a relentless cycle of instability—always searching for a way out, yet finding himself right back where he started.

This Too Shall Pass

Our family's stories are not isolated narratives but interconnected journeys shaped by shared circumstances. When our dad's business collapsed, the economic shockwave rippled through each of our lives, altering every family member's relationship with work and opportunity. When our mom's health failed at her workplace, we all recalibrated our lives—some quitting jobs, others working longer hours—to accommodate this new reality of caregiving.

Though these accounts belong to our family, they reflect universal experiences that could belong to any household. Most families contain at least one story that mirrors ours: the self-made success achieved through relentless effort; the financial devastation wrought by economic forces beyond one's control; the struggle to balance work with caring for an ill family member; the challenges of raising children alone on inadequate wages; the exhaustion of juggling education with multiple part-time jobs; or the disorientation of standing at life's crossroads without a clear path forward.

This collection isn't meant to be read sequentially. Feel free to begin with whichever story resonates most strongly with you, or simply explore a single narrative that speaks to your current circumstances. Each chapter stands alone while contributing to a larger tapestry of shared human experience.

Remember these words when the weight of your own journey feels too heavy to bear: *You are not alone in your struggles. And it's not your fault. The circumstances that challenge you are rarely of your own making. And even in the darkest moments of economic uncertainty or professional setback, this too shall pass.*

When I asked my family to share their labor histories for this book, my dad, with remarkable precision, readily recounted his 63-year journey of work. Jiyoung hesitated at first, unwilling to revisit that time, but eventually opened up when I pressed her. Afterward, we shared a drink together, even though it was only 1 p.m. Yoojung, ever resourceful, supplemented our conversation with drawings and written explanations to fill in any gaps in my understanding. Minjoon downplayed his contributions, embarrassed by what he considered "just part-time work," but stunned me with stories of twelve-hour workdays, with no days off, while still in middle and high school. Jihoon, whom I had approached with the most trepidation, spoke with surprising honesty about his first "income"—a million won earned through illegal online gambling when he was in first grade of middle school.

This process of recording our labor histories became an excavation of our family's most vulnerable memories. Each interview unearthed layers of struggle, resilience, and quiet dignity that had often gone unacknowledged. I am profoundly grateful to my family for their willingness to revisit these painful experiences, for consenting to these interviews, and for entrusting me with their stories for publication. Their continued diligence and perseverance in the face of adversity remains both a comfort and an inspiration.

Though these pages recount my family's collective labor experience, this is ultimately my story. I found the courage to share these narratives through the unwavering love and trust of my family, along with the support and encouragement of friends and colleagues. It is because of this community that I was able to maintain hope in a world that often seems indifferent to individual struggle. To the friends who helped me envision and work toward a more equitable world we could create together, I offer my deepest gratitude.

At one time, owning a small shop in Sadang-dong was the working poor's dream—a pathway to stability. But today, even that modest aspiration is out of reach. Without substantial capital, becoming a shop owner is nearly impossible. And even if one manages to open a rice store, a mom-and-pop shop, a briquette stand, or a beauty salon, it no longer guarantees a way out of poverty. The diverse small shops that once lined the narrow hillside alleys of Sadang-dong's Daldongne have all but disappeared.

(...)

At one time, owning a small shop in Sadang-dong was the working poor's dream—a pathway to stability. But today, even that modest aspiration is out of reach. Without substantial capital, becoming a shop owner is nearly impossible. And even if one manages to open a rice store, a mom-and-pop shop, a briquette stand, or a beauty salon, it no longer guarantees a way out of poverty. The diverse small shops that once lined the narrow hillside alleys of

Sadang-dong's Daldongne have all but disappeared.

— Cho Eun, Sadang-dong Plus 25

Chapter 1: Youngsoo Kang

From Factory Owner to Courier Driver: The Rise and Fall of a Self-Made Entrepreneur

My Dad, Youngsoo, began working at the age of 11, before he had even completed primary school. His career spanned more than six decades, only coming to an end when the COVID-19 pandemic forced him to retire at the age of 72. His career can be divided into three distinct phases: first as a street vendor and factory worker (ages 11-27), then as a successful business owner (ages 28-48), and finally as a motorcycle courier (ages 50-72) after losing everything in the Asian Financial Crisis of 1997.

Starting as a poor young man in the city, my dad achieved his dream of owning a bag factory in his 20s, becoming a symbol of self-made success. However, the economic crisis of the late 1990s destroyed everything he had built. And the world had changed. Unlike in his youth, hard work alone was no longer enough to lift him out of hardship. He concluded his working life in 2020 as a motorcycle courier, unable to realize his final entrepreneurial ambition of owning his own delivery service company.

Profile

- Name : Youngsoo Kang
- Birth Year : 1949
- Education : Incomplete elementary school
- Work Experience : 63 years
- Started Working At : 11 years old
- Occupation History : Street vendor, factory worker, factory owner, wholesale business owner, motorcycle courier, etc.

Early Years: The Factory Worker

Youngsoo's father (my grandfather) was not a rich man, but he was a respected figure in the country community. His mother also completed primary school, which was rare in those days, and taught her children to read and write herself. But their lives took a sudden turn when the family went bankrupt overnight, forcing my grandfather to leave his hometown.

A Poor Boy in the City

In the winter of 1959, my eleven-year-old Dad was brought to Seoul from the countryside by my grandfather before he had even finished primary school. They found shelter in a makeshift dwelling—a small corner of an acquaintance's house, little more than a tent with an open view of the sky. It was a common sight among the urban poor of that era.

At the time, the electricity supply was unreliable—if one neighborhood had power, another would be in the dark, and vice versa. Candles were essential, and my grandfather started making them at home. My Dad helped his father, buying supplies and selling the candles door-to-door. This marked the beginning of his working life.

After two years, as the electricity situation improved, candle sales dwindled. My grandfather had to find a new way to earn money. He set up a stall on the street and opened a comic book rental shop. My Dad helped by lending out comics and selling snacks.

Once the shop provided a stable income, my grandfather bought a house on the top of a mountain in Bukaehyun-dong and brought the rest of the family from the countryside to Seoul. It had been three years since they first moved to the city.

However, their stability proved short-lived. In the 1960s, Seoul underwent massive urban renewal projects. Within a year of the family's reunion, their home and shop were demolished in the name of progress. Overnight, everything they had worked for and owned was gone.

My grandfather opened a small shop, but it struggled to stay afloat. To help make ends meet, my Dad and his siblings sold candy and snacks on the streets. They also took on various hard labor, such as carrying water and waste, hauling rice bags, and pushing wheelbarrows.

Being hungry was the hardest thing for my Dad.

The Apprentice Years at the Bag Factory

Each child in the family took a different path to ease the household's burden. My Dad's oldest brother enlisted in the military, removing one mouth to feed. His second oldest brother, known for his skillful hands, became an apprentice at a TV and radio repair shop. Though the position offered no immediate pay, it provided valuable expertise, allowing him to eventually open his own repair shop. At sixteen, my Dad was introduced to a bag factory by a neighbor. The job offered no salary at first, but it provided room and board, along with the hope of developing his skills as a bag maker.

> *"Back then, we didn't think in terms of salary," my Dad recalls. "Having food to eat and a place to sleep was enough. We set up makeshift sleeping quarters next to the factory, separated only by a curtain. When you're that poor, just having meals and shelter feels like a blessing."*

The factory, located in Seoul's bustling Jongno district near University Road, employed about fifty workers organized into teams of fifteen. Each team reflected a hierarchy: three to four unskilled apprentices like my Dad who handled basic tasks like gluing and sanding, seven to eight intermediate craftsmen, and five to six master craftsmen.

My Dad worked in the section that made large trunks, such as those used for weddings. These bags were 90% handmade, with each piece taking a week to complete. His job was to sew the pockets together. The *oyabung* (a term meaning "boss" or "leader," borrowed from Japanese during the colonial era) would take the finished bags to the market, where they were so popular they sold almost immediately. It was a rewarding feeling.

A First Salary

My Dad worked in a higher-level department at the factory. The business was doing well financially and frequently hosted company dinners for the employees. His skills steadily improved, and after about a year of apprenticeship, he finally began receiving a salary.

"After about a year of hard work and proving myself, the boss finally started paying me a salary. It was only around 10,000 to 15,000 won a month—just enough to scrape by. Still, I was thrilled to be earning my own money," my Dad recalls.

The factory ran on regular shifts, but overtime was common. Workers often stayed late, sometimes until midnight or even dawn. My Dad, always willing to work extra hours, was driven by the higher pay rates.

It had been three years since he started working at the bag factory, and by this time, his salary had increased. Until then, he had been living and eating in a small space next to the factory, where he had hung a curtain to create a makeshift room. While living there wasn't particularly uncomfortable, he began to miss his mother (my grandmother) and decided it was time to start commuting from home.

My Dad asked his father for permission to live at home, and his father agreed, saying, "You can manage your own paycheck, but you'll have to pay for your own food." And so, my Dad began commuting from home. To save on bus fare, he walked several miles each day from his home at the top of Bukaehyun-dong to the factory in Jongno 5-ga.

During this time, my Dad also tried to continue his education by attending night school.

Not long after, his father passed away before reaching fifty. By then, the eldest brother had married and moved out after completing his military service, while the second brother was living at his technical school. This left my Dad, still a teenager, responsible for his mother and younger siblings in their small, single-room dwelling.

Becoming a Craftsman

After six years at the bag factory, my Dad had worked his way up to become a mid-level craftsman. When a coworker tipped him off about better wages elsewhere, he made the pivotal decision to join Samyung Chemical.

Located in Yeongdeungpo, Samyung Chemical was a major export company with 200 employees. Recently, it had expanded into bag manufacturing. The company's bag division was organized into five teams, and my Dad's skills earned him a position as team leader, where he supervised ten workers. His base salary ranged from 150,000 to 200,000 won, and with performance bonuses and incentives, he could earn up to 300,000 won a month—a significant improvement over his previous wages.

The factory operated on a strict, deadline-driven system, with production quotas that had to be met by specific dates. Management fostered competition between the five teams, evaluating them on quantity, speed, and quality. Top-performing teams received rewards and bonuses.

Under my Dad's leadership, his team consistently remained in the upper ranks, though they didn't always secure first place.

"I operated the sewing machines," my Dad recalls. "Whether due to my work ethic or natural dexterity, I excelled. While my team didn't always come in first place, we were always among the top performers."

Many of my Dad's colleagues lived alone near the factory. After work, he would often visit their homes, where they would mostly play games. When my Dad spoke about gambling, I expected to hear stories of big wins or losses. However, my Dad was a 'master of money' in these games—he didn't just play; he made money from them.

"As factory workers, we hadn't learned anything special," my Dad admits. "In our free time, the only thing we could do was go out or gamble. I found my niche in money lending rather than gambling. I'd lend 100,000 won and collect 110,000 won when they

Wages, Performance Bonuses, and the Price of Overtime

Unlike the small, family-owned factory where he had worked before, Samyung Chemical had a more structured corporate environment with regulated hours. However, my Dad often stayed late to earn extra money. When security guards insisted on turning off the lights, his response was always the same: "Just a little longer, I'll finish this and go."

My Dad's drive for overtime work carried complicated implications. As a team leader, his decision to work late meant the entire team had to stay as well. This created tension within the group. Without the extra hours, they would only receive base pay—barely enough to support a family. When wages fell short, workers would leave the factory, leading to understaffing, which made it even harder to meet production targets. And if targets weren't met, they wouldn't get paid. It was a vicious cycle.

After three years, my Dad witnessed the company's decline. Export orders steadily decreased, leading to workforce reductions and cuts in both performance bonuses and base wages.

This local downturn was a reflection of a larger global crisis. In 1973, the First Oil Crisis—triggered by conflicts in the Middle East—sent shockwaves through the world economy, causing manufacturing costs to skyrocket. The United States saw its economic growth plummet from 5.8% in 1973 to negative growth in 1974 and 1975, as documented by the National Bureau of

Economic Research (NBER). South Korea, heavily reliant on exports, also experienced a sharp slowdown, with its growth rate dropping from 14.9% in 1973 to 7.8% by 1975, according to World Bank reports.

In 1974, my Dad left Samyung Chemical and joined Myeongseong Industries in search of better pay. As a highly skilled craftsman, he was well-respected and in demand, always receiving favorable treatment wherever he worked.

A Master Craftsman

Myeongseong Industries was located in Itaewon, behind the Hamilton Hotel. Here, my Dad served as both the factory foreman and dormitory director, roles that significantly expanded his responsibilities. During this time, he met my Mom through a mutual connection. She, too, was a highly skilled technician, having spent over a decade working at a sewing machine factory in the industrial Guro district.

About six months into his position at Myeongseong, my Dad received an offer from Sebel, a German company operating in Korea. Originally focused on wig manufacturing—one of Korea's major exports in the 1970s—Sebel was now expanding into handbag production and needed experienced technicians.

Leveraging his professional network, my Dad collaborated with four former team leaders from Samyung Chemical to negotiate with Sebel. By offering to bring in 30 skilled workers, he strengthened his bargaining position and secured an attractive compensation package: a base salary of 300,000 won, along with performance bonuses.

"When Sebel approached me about their need for bag craftsmen, they asked how many workers I could bring. I told them I could recruit up to 100, depending on the compensation package. At the time, Sebel's factory hadn't even been built yet. I negotiated a base salary of 300,000 won, plus performance incentives," he recalls.

Jeon Taeil and My Dad: Two Paths in an Era of Labor Struggle

Jeon Taeil was a South Korean labor activist who fought against the harsh conditions faced by factory workers. As a garment worker in Seoul's industrial district, he witnessed the brutal exploitation of laborers—long hours, meager wages, and unsafe environments. He became a fierce advocate for labor rights, exposing the inhumane treatment of workers, particularly women, and demanding better working conditions.

Born in 1949, my Dad was a contemporary of Jeon Taeil, who was born just a year earlier in 1948. While Jeon led protests in the garment industry, my Dad worked in bag manufacturing.

"I knew about Jeon Taeil from the news," my Dad recalls. "He was leading protests in Cheonggyecheon. But I saw demonstrations as something for educated people—college students. I

didn't think it was a good idea. I believed that hard work was the solution, that things would improve through perseverance."

On November 13, 1970, at just 22 years old, Jeon Taeil set himself on fire in front of a government building in Seoul, holding a sign that read, "Workers, unite for your rights!" His tragic sacrifice drew national attention to the plight of factory workers and ignited a movement for labor reform in South Korea. Today, he is remembered as a symbol of the fight for workers' rights, and his legacy continues to inspire labor activists both in Korea and beyond.

The Photographer Sideline

The transition to Sebel brought an unexpected challenge for my Dad. While he was a skilled bag technician, Sebel specialized in handbags—a craft that required a completely different set of techniques. He had mastered the art of crafting large bags and cases, but handbag production demanded intricate detailing.

"The techniques are completely different," he explains. "I could work quickly, but my error rate was too high." Struggling to keep up with the new demands, he fell behind in performance and lost the opportunity to earn incentives.

Next to the bag factory where my Dad worked was a wig factory with about 300 female employees. When he first mentioned this, I expected a romance story—but I was mistaken. Instead, my dad noticed that these young women were eager to capture their lives and friendships. At a time when personal cameras were rare, professional portraits were both a luxury and a necessity—something to preserve memories or send home to family.

Seeing an opportunity, he made a bold investment in a Canon camera and became the factory's unofficial photographer. He carved out a side business in the margins of his workday— taking portraits during lunch breaks, dinner hours, and any free moment he could find. Demand exceeded his expectations. Lines formed during every break, and through this unexpected venture, he was able to compensate for his lost performance bonuses—at times even matching his regular salary.

A Home of His Own

Having worked in a bag factory since the age of sixteen, my Dad spent a decade honing his craft and saving diligently. By 1975, after ten years of relentless effort, his discipline paid off. With 3 million won in savings, he purchased a house on a hillside in Bukaehyeon-dong.

The significance of this achievement becomes clearer when considering his housing history. When he first arrived in Seoul, he lived in a tent with his father, pitched in the corner of an acquaintance's yard. Over the years, he moved from one temporary space to another—curtained-off sections next to factory floors, factory dormitories, and a single rented room shared with his mother and siblings. Yet through all these years of instability, one dream remained constant: owning a real home.

By twenty-seven, he had achieved what many thought impossible for someone from his background.

"I saved about 90% of everything I earned," he recalls. "I had a clear goal: buying a house. And I believed that hard work would lead to something better."

The house had six rooms and a spacious courtyard. One room was shared by his mother and siblings, while another became his own—and later, his and my Mom's. To generate extra income, he rented out a third room. Over time, he set up a tent in the courtyard to start his own bag factory, where some of his workers also lived. The house became more than just a home—it was the foundation of both his family and his business, marking a turning point in his journey toward stability and success.

How My Dad Bought a House at 27

Growing up in poverty and living in a tent because his family couldn't afford proper housing, my Dad's dream was always to buy a home.

With only an elementary school education and a family to support, he faced immense challenges. In his first year at the bag factory, he didn't even receive a wage. But through relentless hard work, discipline, and sacrifice, he saved obsessively—putting aside nearly every won he earned. After a decade of determination, he finally achieved what once seemed impossible: he bought a house.

His personal journey coincided with South Korea's dramatic economic transformation. When he entered the workforce in the 1960s, the country was undergoing rapid industrialization. GDP growth, which had been below 4%, surged to 8.4% in the 1960s and 9.0% in the 1970s. The manufacturing sector—

where my Dad built his career—thrived, growing at an impressive 16.8% in the 1960s and 15.8% in the 1970s. Jobs were plentiful, and workers could seek better opportunities by switching employers.

Wage growth during this era was equally remarkable. After enduring a year without pay at the bag factory, my Dad's wages steadily increased as his skills improved. Labor activist Jeon Taeil's case, studied by Professor Park Kisung of Sungshin Women's University, provides a useful reference. In his analysis *Unenforceable Labor Standards Laws Killed Jeon Taeil*, Park noted that Jeon's monthly wage increased from 1,500 won in 1965 to 23,000 won by 1970—15.3 times higher in nominal terms and 7.6 times higher in real terms, after adjusting for inflation.

Starting from a lower wage base, wage increases tend to be more pronounced. If I were to calculate my Dad's wage growth in this way, it would amount to several hundred times his initial earnings. While this calculation has its limitations, his steadily rising income, combined with his growing expertise and experience, helped him gain financial stability and plan for the future.

Professor Park further notes: "In 1970, the average monthly salary for a male journalist was 22,700 won, and for a male teacher, 37,200 won. Considering that both professions required higher education and were typically held by older individuals, Jeon Taeil's wage of 23,000 won per month as a 22-year-old elementary school dropout wasn't low."

Education played a key role in determining wages, and my Dad, having dropped out of elementary school, faced challenges in securing stable employment. However, at the time, practical skills and hands-on experience were highly valued, opening doors for workers like him who lacked formal education but had strong technical expertise.

Today, such a path to homeownership seems nearly impossible. According to 2022 data from the Korea Real Estate Agency, the lowest 20% of income earners in Seoul would need to save for an entire century—without spending a single won—just to afford a home in the top 20% price range. The rate of increase in real estate prices has far outpaced wage growth, making it unthinkable for a worker today to buy a house even if they saved 100% of their salary for 10 years, as my Dad once did.

My Dad's first home purchase was possible not just because of his unwavering discipline and determination, but also because of an economic environment that supported workers. Factors like abundant job opportunities, systematic promotions, steady wage increases, and relatively affordable housing prices made homeownership a realistic goal for those willing to put in the effort. His story serves as a reminder of how much the landscape has changed for today's workers.

Becoming an Entrepreneur

A Bag Factory Boss

From the moment he bought his house, my Dad had a clear vision: he wanted to start his own factory. Many of his coworkers had already taken the leap, launching their own operations. In 1976, he followed suit, quitting his job at Sebel to establish a bag factory in his backyard, housed under a simple tent.

Transitioning from factory worker to factory owner, he started with just two sewing machines and a small team of four or five employees. To understand market trends, he visited retail stores, carefully analyzing their best-selling items. His strategy was straightforward yet effective—replicating popular designs with slight modifications and pricing them 10–20% below market rates.

He also introduced a unique product that set him apart: a three-tier bag set featuring small, medium, and large bags that nested inside one another. The concept resonated with value-conscious consumers, offering three bags for the price of one in a compact, space-saving package. This innovation, combined with his keen market instincts, helped lay the foundation for his growing business.

The White Phone: A Status Symbol

The bag factory flourished, with orders pouring in faster than my Dad could fulfill them. No sooner had he delivered a batch to a store than another order for 50 more came in. Each production cycle took three days to cut and assemble, generating a net profit of 100,000 to 200,000 won—equivalent to about a month's salary at the time.

"I paid my workers more than other factories," he admitted, "but I also made them work hard."

As demand grew, retailers frequently complained that they couldn't place new orders because they had no way to reach him. This led to a major investment: a white phone—a privately owned telephone line that could be bought and sold, unlike the "blue phones" whose ownership wasn't transferable. At the time, a white phone was so valuable that it could be worth more than a house. With this new lifeline for business communication, orders increased, and the factory expanded to 10 employees.

After four to five years, the factory's hilltop location in Bukaehyeon-dong became a major obstacle. The lack of vehicle access made it difficult to receive supplies and distribute products efficiently. To solve this, my Dad invested 5 million won in a new property near Bukaehyeon-dong's northwest gate. The new location provided better accessibility for vehicles, a larger workspace, and closer proximity to key business districts—streamlining logistics and opening the door for further expansion.

With a solid production system in place, my Dad shifted his focus from manufacturing to business development. He began visiting bag shops regularly to observe trends and build relationships with store clerks. Over meals, he gathered valuable insights on inventory levels and sales patterns, refining his strategy to stay ahead of market demand. Over the next two to three years, these efforts laid the groundwork for even greater growth.

The Shifting Marketplace

The 1980s ushered in a period of social transformation in South Korea. Curfews were lifted, and restrictions on school uniforms and student hairstyles were relaxed. With color television becoming widespread and newspapers printing in color, a new consumer culture took shape. As noted in *Advertising, Reading the Times* (2007), "The items consumed and the way of life itself became incomparably more diverse than in previous periods. As a result, the 1980s saw the establishment of a consumer culture fundamentally different from that of earlier decades."

This cultural shift brought a crisis to my Dad's factory. Demand had moved toward fashionable, branded bags, making his durable, no-frills designs less popular in an increasingly brand-conscious market. Sales declined, and my Mom, who had been cooking meals for more than 10 workers, was struggling to keep up.

"I never considered expanding the factory," my Dad reflected. "Other manufacturers were developing their own trademarks and original designs, but I was still just copying existing products. As consumers started seeking designer brands over simple, affordable bags, I found myself falling behind the times."

Realizing the changing market dynamics, my Dad downsized the factory and relocated it to Seogyo-dong. Though work remained, shrinking profit margins made it difficult to sustain the business. Eventually, he made the difficult decision to close the factory and move to Mangwon-dong.

In Mangwon-dong, he shifted his focus from manufacturing to distribution. Instead of producing bags himself, he subcontracted a factory to manufacture them and sold the finished products to retailers. During the back-to-school season, shoe bags became his bestsellers. To maximize sales, he placed large orders through his subcontractor and supplied them to bag stores while also setting up a market stall to sell directly to customers.

Then, in 1984, disaster struck. Mangwon-dong, a low-lying area near the Han River, had long been prone to flooding during monsoon season. Despite rapid urbanization in the 1960s and 1970s, the drainage system remained inadequate, allowing floodwaters to accumulate quickly during heavy rains. That year, the reservoir bank in Mangwon-dong burst, inundating more than 5,000 homes across Mangwon-dong, Seogyo-dong, Seongsan-dong, and Hapjeong-dong. My Dad's house was among those submerged, and the bags he had stored inside were completely ruined.

With his inventory destroyed and no way to recover, the flood brought his decade-long business to an end, marking the conclusion of my Dad's journey as a bag manufacturer and distributor.

Finding New Ground in Wholesale

After the loss of his manufacturing business, my Dad found a new opportunity in Cheonggyecheon's 8th Street, the heart of the bag-making supply chain. He leased a small shop and transitioned from manufacturing to wholesale, establishing himself as a zipper supplier.

"Success was almost guaranteed," my Dad recalls. "I had built strong relationships with so many bag factory owners over the years, and they stood by me through thick and thin."

His deep industry experience proved invaluable. Years of running his own factory had given him direct access to top suppliers, allowing him to source high-quality materials at competitive prices. His network of fellow bag makers became loyal customers, ensuring steady sales. With even one major factory as a client, he knew he could build a sustainable and profitable business.

A Sharp Business Mind

My Dad was a sharp businessman who understood the challenges small bag factories faced, particularly their struggles with cash flow. To support them, he offered materials like zippers on credit, a strategy that not only built trust but also secured a loyal customer base.

Manufacturing bags required multiple materials—fabric, zippers, and bond. While my Dad primarily sold zippers, he also sourced fabric, jacquard, and bond from a nearby supplier, reselling them at a 10–20% markup. This allowed him to earn a brokerage profit while providing bag makers with the convenience of purchasing all necessary materials from a single supplier.

"There were very few cash transactions back then. Instead, we used promissory notes to make purchases and settle debts."

Promissory notes served as financial commitments, where one party pledged to pay a certain amount or entrusted payment to a third party. Unlike the structured commercial paper system in the U.S., which large corporations used to raise capital, promissory notes in Korea were more informal, relying heavily on personal and business relationships.

Wholesalers issued promissory notes to the factories supplying bag materials, and bag factories issued promissory notes to wholesalers when purchasing materials. These notes typically matured in three to six months. According to the article *Addressing the Growing Problem of Commercial Paper Transactions*, the proportion of commercial paper transactions among small and medium-sized businesses increased from

45.6% in 1988 to 59.2% in 1992. Although the statutory maturity period for commercial paper was 60 days, 60% of issued notes had terms of 90 days or longer. By 1998, the average payment term had stretched beyond 120 days.

However, material suppliers needed cash to keep production running. To bridge the gap, they relied on commercial paper discounting, selling promissory notes to financial institutions at a discount—effectively paying interest upfront to receive cash immediately.

Rather than using promissory notes, my Dad took a different approach. He paid for materials in cash, negotiating a 3% discount—the same fee material suppliers would have lost had they discounted the notes. This strategy allowed him to acquire materials at a lower cost while maintaining strong relationships with suppliers, further reinforcing his reputation as a savvy and reliable businessman.

Note Warigang: Usurious Lending through Bill Discounting

My Dad took things a step further. At the time, South Korea's traditional banking system was notoriously exclusionary, making it difficult for small businesses to access formal financial services. As he often recounted, securing a loan required personal connections with a bank manager, and even then, banks demanded a 3% commission just to process the application—a barrier that kept most small businesses shut out of conventional credit channels.

Issuing commercial paper was an even greater privilege, reserved for only the most established businesses. In Dongdaemun Market, Seoul's bustling commercial hub, fewer than ten out of hundreds of wholesalers met the stringent requirements—large bank deposits and flawless financial records. My Dad's business was one of the select few qualified to issue commercial paper. Recognizing this advantage, he began issuing commercial paper on behalf of smaller merchants, charging a commission for the service.

Amid this flawed financial landscape, the term *Note Warigang* emerged as a local expression for usurious lending through bill discounting—a practice that became a vital lifeline for small merchants.

Having operated his store in the same location for over a decade, my Dad developed a deep understanding of the local business environment. He knew the financial health of neighboring stores and had a keen sense of each merchant's creditworthiness. This insight allowed him to expand into a form of informal banking, where he would convert commercial paper into cash for merchants in urgent need of funds, earning a commission in the process.

A Study on the Improvement of the Commercial Paper System and the Role of Credit Insurance System

Tak Gunjin (2004)

Commercial paper became deeply ingrained in the fabric of Korean business for several key reasons. At the time, most Korean companies lacked the capital for cash transactions. Even large corporations, when they had available cash, often leveraged their market position by paying with commercial paper. Smaller businesses, in turn, accepted this system because they could convert the papers into cash before maturity through a process known as "discounting," and the bank-based collection system was relatively convenient.

For small and medium-sized businesses with limited collateral, commercial paper served as a vital financial lifeline. Since it typically circulated among companies with established trading relationships, it offered significant advantages over traditional financing options—no collateral was required, and costly credit checks could be avoided.

However, the true vulnerabilities of this system became evident during the IMF crisis of the late 1990s. What had once seemed like an efficient financial tool revealed its darker side: when major companies failed, they triggered a devastating domino effect. Even well-managed businesses found themselves caught in the financial turmoil, exposing the systemic risks of the system.

The interconnected nature of these financial relationships posed particular challenges. Most companies built their cash flow management around commercial papers, which would often change hands multiple times as a form of payment. While regulations technically limited endorsements to three transfers, businesses frequently bypassed these limits using various workarounds. This meant that if any single company in the chain faltered, it could trigger a cascade of financial failures, affecting numerous other businesses.

The system had evolved far beyond its original purpose of facilitating credit between businesses. During economic downturns, when defaults on these notes increased, even healthy small and medium-sized enterprises could face bankruptcy—not due to poor management, but because of their position within this complex web of financial obligations.

A Complex System of Credit and Delayed Payments

The financial relationship between my Dad's store, the bag factory, and the material factory was built on a complex system of credit and delayed payments. The bag factory could obtain materials from my Dad's shop simply by recording the amount in their books, essentially buying on credit. On the 25th of each month, my Dad would tally up their purchases. The bag factory would then pay 30% of the total amount in cash, with the remaining 70% settled through promissory notes maturing in three to six months. For instance, if the total amount was 10 million won, the bag factory would pay 3 million won in cash and cover the remaining 7 million won with promissory notes.

This system created a cash flow gap for my Dad—he would provide the materials on credit, meaning there was a one-month delay before receiving any cash. Moreover, another gap of three to six months occurred before he could cash in on the promissory notes.

This cycle repeated every month, creating a snowball effect. For example, if the bag factory spent another 10 million won the following month, they would again pay just 30% in cash, with another promissory note for the balance. As a result, the outstanding notes grew exponentially: 7 million won the first month, 14 million won the second month, and 21 million won the third month. Some notes could be cashed after three months, while others took six months to mature.

When my Dad received notes from the bag factory instead of cash, he had to issue his own notes to purchase materials from suppliers. As the bag factory's debt to him grew, so did his obligations to his suppliers. Each month on the 25th, he would scramble to cover his own notes using whatever cash he received from the bag factory, combined with his available funds.

Initially, having 30 to 50 million won in monthly cash flow was sufficient to maintain this system. However, over time, the required amount ballooned to 70-80 million won.

My Dad found himself trapped in a precarious cycle. To collect the money he had extended on credit to the bag factory and cash in the promissory notes he received from them, he had to keep supplying them with materials. In turn, to secure these materials, he needed to continue issuing his own promissory notes to his suppliers. There was no way to break free from this system. The issuance of bills was entirely based on credit, and any sign of financial strain would immediately halt his ability to issue notes, putting the entire operation at risk of collapse.

"Managing these monthly note payments became more crucial than actually running the business," he explained, emphasizing how this financial juggling act had come to dominate his business life.

Declaring Bankruptcy

The first warning signs emerged in 1995, when one or two promissory notes from the bag factory started to bounce. Then came the devastating blow—his largest customer, the bag factory, declared bankruptcy. Outstanding debts in the tens of millions of won became uncollectible overnight.

As my Dad's business floundered, the burden of his own issued notes grew heavier, with mounting interest compounding the strain.

While he fought to keep the business afloat, another significant blow struck. Roughly six months later, a second major customer, another bag factory, filed for bankruptcy. This double catastrophe proved to be too much for the business to withstand.

By July 1996, the intricate financial house of cards finally collapsed. My father could no longer cover the promissory notes he had issued.

This marked the beginning of a larger economic crisis in South Korea. Following my Dad's bankruptcy, South Korea was hit by the 1997 Asian financial crisis, which plunged the country into a state of near-bankruptcy. The crisis left 4 out of 10 households grappling with unemployment or bankruptcy.

The Fall: How the Economic Crisis Shattered a Middle-Class Dream

My Dad's rise to success mirrored South Korea's own economic miracle. After becoming president of a bag factory in 1976, he achieved symbols of status that once seemed unimaginable—like owning a white phone worth as much as a house and being the first in the neighborhood to own a color television.

Despite a brief setback in the 1980s when the market shifted, he reinvented himself as a wholesale supplier of bag materials. By 1986, he owned a comfortable 1,600-square-foot apartment in Dapsimli and two cars. His prosperity allowed for middle-class luxuries like golf and scuba diving. He had achieved the quintessential Korean dream, rising from urban poverty to comfortable middle-class stability. However, the IMF crisis proved insurmountable, and his financial security crumbled, leaving him impoverished once again.

When my Dad's business failed in 1996, I initially believed it was unrelated to the IMF crisis that would soon hit South Korea in 1997. I attributed his bankruptcy to personal failings—perhaps greed or mismanagement. However, historical records tell a different story. The warning signs of the looming financial turmoil—slowing growth, declining exports, and rising external debt—were already evident in 1996. A January 1997 article in the Korea Economic Daily highlighted a sobering statistic: over 19,000 small and medium-sized businesses had failed the previous year. Many of these failures were not caused by poor management or lack of sales, but by a devastating chain reaction set off by worthless promissory notes—each default triggering the next in a cruel domino effect. The core issue was that these notes had lost their value, transforming from financial instruments into little more than worthless paper.

It wasn't just the failure of his business that left him penniless. After the bankruptcy, my Dad found himself stripped bare once again. Yet, he still believed, as he had before, that he could rebuild. But this time, things were different. It wasn't like 30 years ago.

His age became a barrier, as he was approaching 50. His skills no longer aligned with the evolving market, and his professional network had crumbled. The bag manufacturing industry, once his livelihood, was in decline, with many companies either folding or relocating operations overseas to cut labor costs in the aftermath of the crisis. Retraining for a new career seemed unattainable, and returning to his previous industry was no longer a viable option.

Family obligations added to the burden. My Mom, who had been a homemaker for two decades, reentered the workforce but could only secure low-paying jobs. While my sister

Yoojung was married and independent, my sister Jiyoung and I, aged 20 and 16, still relied on our parents for support.

On top of everything else, my Dad was burdened with debt. Failing in business doesn't just mean going from 100 to 0; it means dropping to -200. A significant portion of the money he earned had to be used to pay off the debts he had accumulated.

Our family's struggle in the aftermath of bankruptcy became a long, difficult journey through hardship—a story shared by many middle-class Korean families caught in the economic turmoil of the late 1990s.

The statistics reflect a story that mirrors my Dad's experience. Research by Eunyoung Nam (2009, *"Polarization of Classes after the Global Financial Crisis: Changes in Daily Life and Consumption"*) showed that 41% of middle-class Koreans lost their status after the financial crisis. The impact wasn't random; it hit certain groups harder than others. Among those who fell out of the middle class, 61.8% were aged 40 or older, disproportionately affecting older individuals. In contrast, 58.2% of those who maintained their middle-class status had a university degree or higher. Conversely, 56.1% of those who dropped out of the middle class had only a high school education or less. My Dad, at 48 years old with only an elementary school education, perfectly embodied these risk factors.

The aftermath of the Asian financial crisis reshaped South Korea's economic landscape. The country not only grappled with widespread unemployment but also witnessed a fundamental shift in the nature of work. The new economy prioritized "labor flexibility"—a term that masked the rise of temporary, contract, and dispatched positions, offering less job security and stability. Despite my Dad's determination and strong work ethic, these structural changes pushed him into the growing ranks of the "working poor," where low wages and job insecurity became his daily reality.

My once-successful Dad, a former business owner who had employed others, spent the next

two decades of his life working as a motorcycle
courier driver.

Starting Over at Fifty: Life as a Motorcycle Courier Driver

My Dad entered the motorcycle courier industry in 1998 at the age of 50 and continued working in it until he was 72. It was the COVID-19 pandemic that finally led him to stop, as the demand for his services significantly decreased.

A Motorcycle Courier Driver: A New Chapter of Hard Work and Survival

The motorcycle courier industry, introduced from Japan in the early 1990s, initially focused on package deliveries for errand centers and wholesale markets. As demand increased throughout the late 1990s, the industry expanded rapidly.

My Dad stumbled upon the motorcycle courier job by chance. One day, he saw a street advertisement for motorcycle courier drivers and walked into a courier service office in Yongsan, marking the beginning of his new career. Having frequently used his motorcycle to transport goods while working at the bag factory, he was already confident in his riding skills.

His first workplace was modest, with only seven or eight drivers. The young owner ran the business, while his wife handled delivery orders over the phone. My Dad made five to six deliveries a day, earning between 70,000 and 80,000 won. Due to the small size of the operation, there was limited work available.

Courier drivers were required to pay a daily "trip fee"—an attendance fee for the right to work, regardless of whether they received any deliveries. At this office, the trip fee was 10,000 won per day. Eager to earn more, my Dad was willing to pay the trip fee and take on as many deliveries as possible.

My Dad explained, "The work is tough, so many people only last a day and never return.

That's why the shop owner collects an advance payment from the delivery drivers for the month. Some customers pay by card, while corporate clients settle on a monthly basis. The shop pays drivers at the end of the month, deducting the trip fees. If a driver's earnings don't cover the trip fee, they end up owing the owner the difference."

After about two years, my Dad switched to another courier company in search of better earnings—a move that mirrored his earlier career transitions in the bag industry, always in pursuit of slightly higher pay. The parallel wasn't lost on him; whether at age 20 or 50, his motivation remained the same: survival through hard work.

The Cost of Making More

The new courier service where my Dad worked was larger than his previous job, employing 25 to 30 drivers. The owner, slightly younger than my Dad, ran the operation. However, with this larger operation came increased costs.

The daily trip fee rose to 12,000 won, 2,000 won more than his previous shop. Additionally, drivers were required to provide customers with 1,000-won discount coupons for each delivery as a "promotional fee." This meant that a 10,000-won delivery would actually earn only 9,000 won before further deductions.

Despite these added expenses, the workload was substantial. My Dad made about 10 deliveries a day. While the physical toll was heavy, his earnings could exceed 100,000 won.

The delivery assignment system operated through a name tag board—drivers would hang their tags upon arrival, and deliveries were assigned in that order. My Dad arrived at work at 7:00 a.m. to ensure he could be the first to hang his name tag, thus guaranteeing at least one additional delivery.

While assignments were primarily based on the order of name tags, there was also a human element. The phone operators, who took orders and assigned deliveries, wielded considerable influence. They could decide whether a driver received a simple paper delivery or a grueling, low-paying job involving heavy loads. To improve his chances of better assignments, my Dad occasionally treated the dispatchers to drinks.

He also worked late into the night, when the younger drivers had already finished their shifts. By the time he returned home, it was usually around 9 or 10 p.m., when he would finally have dinner.

This routine continued for four to five years, until life took an unexpected turn. My Mom, who worked as janitorial staff, suffered a brain hemorrhage while on the job. It was classified as a workers' compensation case. My Dad left his job as a courier driver to become her full-time caregiver, spending the next three years at her side in the hospital.

The *"Porter"* of Yongsan

While my Dad worked for several quick-service companies, he remained in Yongsan, where the electronics market shaped the nature of deliveries. Unlike typical motorcycle couriers who transported documents or small packages, the riders in Yongsan specialized in delivering heavy electronics such as computers, washing machines, and refrigerators—bulky items that were difficult to transport.

Courier drivers earned little if they made deliveries one at a time, so to maximize their earnings, they needed to handle multiple deliveries simultaneously. To achieve this, my Dad modified his motorcycle by installing an iron pipe in the back and adding wooden planks, transforming his modest vehicle into a makeshift delivery truck.

My Dad lifted the computer, washing machine, and refrigerator—each heavier than he was—and loaded them onto his motorcycle, which was taller than him. He would ride with these heavy appliances, and upon reaching his destination, he would unload them one by one and deliver them to the customer's doorstep.

After gaining insight into the courier industry while working as a truck courier driver, my sister Yoojung remarked grimly, "The Yongsan couriers aren't called drivers—they're called *'porters.'* No one wants to do this work. It's usually left to older men like Dad." But my Dad, unfazed, simply said, "It's like picking up money on the road," doing the kind of work others avoid.

The iron pipe attached to the motorcycle dug into his back while driving. After four or five years, he developed a herniated disk that required surgery, leaving him with permanent weakness in one leg. My Dad also endured multiple accidents while working as a motorcycle courier. He was hospitalized at least once every two to three years.

Return to the Road

In 2007, after three years spent caring for my Mom in the hospital, my parents finally returned home. And my Dad resumed his work as a motorcycle courier.

His new workplace was owned by a familiar face—one of his former colleagues from his earlier courier days, a man a few years younger than him.

The shop consisted of 25 to 30 drivers, ranging in age from their twenties to their sixties, with my Dad among the older group. The daily trip fee remained at 12,000 won, but the promotional discount coupon fee had risen to 1,500 won per delivery.

Corporate clients often settled their accounts on a monthly basis, frequently using gift certificates instead of cash. "The courier service business ran heavily on credit," my Dad explained. "When corporate clients paid their monthly bills with gift certificates, the owner would pass those certificates on to us instead of cash."

After deducting daily trip fees, promotional costs, and fuel expenses, his monthly earnings typically ranged from 2 to 2.5 million won. However, a significant portion—often over 1 million won—came in the form of gift certificates, as many customers paid for deliveries with them, and the courier service accepted them as payment.

Chasing the Owner's Dream: Two Failed Ventures

Like many bag factory workers who dream of owning their own factory, motorcycle couriers often aspire to run their own courier business. My Dad was no exception. Seeing several former colleagues transition from drivers to business owners, he was inspired to follow the same path. However, after two decades as a motorcycle courier, his attempts to open his own shop ended in failure—far more challenging than he had ever anticipated.

"Every courier dreams of becoming an owner," my Dad reflected. "We imagine the owners counting money and managing operations without having to ride a motorcycle themselves."

First Venture: One-Man Operation (1998)

Before taking his first job as a courier, my Dad invested 5 million won to purchase a one-man motorcycle courier business. The deal included the business rights, a phone line with 20 regular clients, a motorcycle, and a company vest—a solid foundation for independence, or so it seemed.

However, running a solo operation proved overwhelming. While serving Customer A, calls from Customer B went unanswered. With no backup or support system in place, clients gradually left, and within a month, my Dad was forced to shut down the business. Accepting the setback, he sought employment at an established courier company.

Second Venture: Full Operation (2012)

Fourteen years after his first attempt, my Dad decided to try again. From a driver's perspective, owning a courier company seemed like an ideal business model:

- Owners could earn without physically laboring—they wouldn't need to ride the motorcycle.

- There was a guaranteed income from drivers' daily trip fees. With 30 drivers, owners could easily earn over 10 million won a month (12,000 won per driver × 30 drivers × 30 days).
- Owners had control over work distribution, giving them significant authority over their drivers.
- Perhaps most appealing, the business required relatively little startup capital compared to other ventures.

However, the hidden costs proved substantial. Successful courier shops often operated as family businesses—the owner maintaining client relationships, his wife handling phone operations and office management, and their children assisting with marketing and flyer distribution.

My Dad, attempting to run the operation alone, quickly found himself overwhelmed. Eventually, after running at a loss, he was forced to sell the business below cost and return once again to working as a driver.

The Gradual Sunset of a Working Life

After my Mom suffered a brain hemorrhage, she was left with right-side paralysis, limited mobility, and an inability to speak. Her condition required round-the-clock care, even after she returned home from the hospital.

My sister Yoojung stayed with our parents, assisting in caring for Mom and offering support. In 2017, she moved out to begin working as a truck courier driver. Meanwhile, my Dad took on the responsibility of caring for Mom, ensuring she had her meals. This made it difficult for him to maintain his previous delivery volume. At 69, his age and reduced capacity to work made the 12,000 won daily trip fee at courier shops a burden.

Yoojung suggested an alternative: the "Integrated Call" service, a delivery order brokerage platform that didn't charge daily trip fees but took a 20% commission per delivery. While high-volume drivers benefited from the flat daily fees at traditional courier shops, the commission-based system offered a more practical option for someone like my Dad, with a reduced workload.

My Dad adapted by focusing on two steady morning deliveries, bringing breakfast to office workers on weekdays. His day began at 5 AM with these deliveries, after which he'd return home to prepare Mom's breakfast. He would then make a few more deliveries through the Integrated Call service until mid-afternoon, returning home by 2 or 3 PM to share lunch with Mom. Later, he discontinued the Integrated Call service, concentrating solely on the steady morning deliveries.

However, the COVID-19 pandemic in 2020 dealt the final blow to his working life. As companies shifted to remote work, his regular breakfast delivery clients disappeared.

At 72, my Dad's career came to an end, marking not only the close of his 20 years as a motorcycle courier but also a remarkable 63-year journey as a worker—one that had begun in his childhood.

An Ongoing Labor

In 2020, at the age of 72, my Dad officially concluded his working life, marking the end of a 63-year journey in paid labor. Now, he stays at home to care for my Mom. While he no longer works in the traditional sense, his life isn't defined by financial struggle.

He owns his home, freeing him from the stress of monthly rent payments, annual increases, and the uncertainty of frequent relocations. The debts from his business failure have long been cleared through his years of hard work as a motorcycle courier, and his children have achieved financial independence.

However, this stability doesn't equate to financial security. My Dad has minimal savings—only a few million won in his bank account—and lacks both a national pension and private insurance. His children's financial support is limited to occasional pocket money on holidays and birthdays.

His current income comes from two sources: the Basic Old Age Pension, a government program for seniors over 65, and a caregiving allowance for tending to my Mom, who is classified as disabled.

In a sense, my Dad's life of work continues. The location has simply shifted from the busy streets of Yongsan to the quieter rooms of his home, where he provides the constant care my Mom needs.

Despite a limp from past injuries, my Dad maintains relatively good health, thanks to his disciplined lifestyle—no drinking, no smoking, and a commitment to regular exercise. This resilience allowed him to work as a motorcycle courier until he was 72, and it now supports him in caring for my Mom.

Yet, there's an undeniable truth we must face: as time passes, age will inevitably catch up with him, limiting his ability to care for her. When that day arrives, my siblings and I will have to make difficult decisions—whether to extend our working hours or even leave our jobs entirely to care for our aging parents. This is the harsh reality of poverty: not only a path filled with obstacles but a minefield where each step could lead to a cascade of impossible choices.

§ *The beginning of this book must be dedicated to my Dad. This isn't simply out of filial piety or respect for his role as the head of our family, but because his labor history speaks to a larger truth. Beginning work at age 11, before even finishing elementary school, he became the first and longest-serving worker in our family.*

His 63-year journey—spanning from child laborer to business owner, from courier to caregiver—deserves recognition and respect, regardless of the wealth he may or may not have accumulated.

Sookhee Choi: Mom

- Born in 1950

In 1967, of the 360,556 girls who graduated from elementary school, only 167,011 continued on to middle school, meaning more than half did not pursue further education. At the time, societal norms and expectations—such as "don't burden your eldest son," "give way to your younger brother," "accept and help your family's poverty," and the belief that "girls don't need education"—served as strong justifications for girls to leave school.

(...)

Teenage girls born in 1954 found themselves working in factories instead. South Korea's economic growth strategy at the time focused on labor-intensive light manufacturing industries like wigs, plywood, textiles, shoes, and electrical appliances. These young female workers endured harsh conditions, living in cramped dormitories partitioned with veneered plywood and commuting long hours to and from work. To cope with the grueling schedules, some resorted to stimulants like "timing" to stay awake. Their low-wage, long-hour labor became the backbone of the country's industrial rise.

Cho Hyungguk, "320,000 daughters were born in 1954," Kyunghyang Shinmun, January 26, 2022.

The Eldest Daughter

My Mom is the eldest of six siblings. Her father (my grandfather) was a kind man, but his fondness for drinking often made it difficult to provide consistently for the family. After finishing elementary school, she chose to work at a sewing machine factory to support her parents and younger siblings. In a photograph capturing a moment of youthful camaraderie with her friends, she stands out as the only one not wearing a school uniform.

She worked tirelessly at the factory, saving money to send her siblings to school and help her mother secure a home. When she got married, she gave all the money she had saved to her mother.

Marriage

At 26, my Mom married my Dad. By then, she was a skilled technician at a garment factory in Guro, where she served as a foreman overseeing several dozen workers. She left her job when she got married. When asked why she married my Dad, she said it was because he had a home and she trusted he would always provide for the family. She believed that with his income, she could live comfortably without needing to work.

As she had hoped, she never returned to the factory after marrying. However, my Dad's bag factory operated out of their home, so her responsibilities were far from over. She raised three children while also feeding over ten factory workers. Without a car, she walked to the market, bought groceries for more than fifteen people, cooked every meal, and washed the dishes. Yet, she wasn't just confined to the kitchen—her husband was the boss, and she was the boss's wife.

Being a stay-at-home mother was her pride. She took deep satisfaction in living off her husband's earnings, seeing not needing to work outside the home as a mark of dignity. So, when my Dad went bankrupt in 1996, losing the house, the car, and the people, she still refused to return to work. Not working was the last dignity she held onto.

Return to Work

A few years after my Dad's bankruptcy, our family was able to secure a small house once again. My Dad started working as a motorcycle courier to make a living, and by then, all of us children had grown up and started our own lives. Only then did my Mom return to work.

At first, she took on a side job at home, gluing eyeballs onto dolls. Later, she found a job at a factory near our house, where she met a Chinese worker—the first foreigner she had ever encountered. She came home, teaching me the Chinese she had learned from her, and began cooking Chinese dishes for us.

Before long, she transitioned to working as a cleaner. Even though she had a job, she remained solely responsible for cooking and managing the household. She found cleaning to be a good fit, as it allowed her to balance work and family responsibilities. Despite waking up at 4 a.m. to catch the first bus, she appreciated being able to finish her day by 3 or 4 p.m.

My Mom was grateful to the office staff in the building she cleaned, appreciating their kind gestures, like offering her drinks or chocolate pies. She took pride in receiving holiday gifts from the company. Above all, she was proud to earn her own money and be recognized for her hard work.

Industrial Accident

After about two years of working as a cleaner, my Mom was found collapsed in the restroom of the company building where she worked. She was 55 years old at the time. The incident was classified as an industrial accident. She underwent major surgery and remained in the hospital for three years. As a result of the aftereffects, she is now paralyzed on her right side, which makes movement difficult and has left her unable to speak.

For 12 years, my eldest sister, Yoojung, lived with and cared for both of our parents. Now, my Dad has taken on the responsibility of caring for my Mom.

§ *I was unable to interview my Mom about her work history. This account is based on my Dad's memories and my own.*

Emotional labor traces a path that mirrors women's positions in the labor market—an arc that is both revealing and bitter.

(...)

In their twenties, women are often valued for their appearance and youth, leading them into front-line sales roles in cosmetics and retail. In their thirties and forties, many juggle work with childcare and are channeled into call centers. By their forties and fifties, having aged out of youth, they move into supermarket sales. And when society no longer demands services tied to freshness, beauty, or cheerful smiles, these women are funneled into roles like cleaning, restaurant work, caregiving, or postpartum care—jobs shaped by expectations of maternal sacrifice.

— Heejeong, *Workers Fall*

Chapter 2: Jiyoung Kang

From Part-Time Hustles to Corporate Stability: A Fight for a Career

In 1996, when my Dad's business went bankrupt, my second-oldest sister, Jiyoung, was preparing to retake her college entrance exams with the goal of becoming a teacher. However, without financial support from home, she spent the next three years juggling various part-time jobs—working as a café server, kitchen assistant, telemarketer, flyer distributor, bookkeeper, and department store sales associate—all while striving to reach her college aspirations. Despite her relentless hard work and determination, her dream remained just out of reach.

Jiyoung eventually decided to find a full-time job, but this was no easy task amid the IMF crisis (Asian Financial Crisis), a period of widespread unemployment in South Korea. Undeterred, she continued working part-time while attending vocational courses to improve her job prospects. Her perseverance paid off in 2000 when she secured a position as an information operator at KT, a public corporation—though it was only a contract position. The company had a program that allowed contract workers to transition into full-time roles. Seizing this opportunity, Jiyoung worked her way up from part-time student to contract worker, and eventually to a full-time employee at a major corporation. Within a year of becoming a full-time employee, she got married and chose to become a full-time homemaker.

Profile

- Name : Jiyoung Kang
- Birth Year : 1977
- Education : General High School Graduate
- Work Experience : 11 years
- Started Working At : 19 years old
- Occupation History : café server, kitchen assistant, telemarketer, flyer distributor, bookkeeper, department store sales associate, information operator, etc.

Path to College

During the winter break following the 1995 college entrance exam, my sister Jiyoung took her first part-time job at Pizza Hut to save money for college application fees. Applying to two or three universities required around 200,000 won, and with the minimum hourly wage at just 1,275 won in 1995, even a full month of full-time work would barely cover the cost.

"My Dad went bankrupt in 1996, and ever since, the atmosphere at home has been heavy," Jiyoung recalled.

December was the busiest season for the pizzeria, and Jiyoung worked as a server at Pizza Hut. Although the job was demanding, there was a silver lining—her hourly wage of 2,000 won was well above the industry standard of 1,400 won. She used her earnings to pay for college applications and attended interviews. Despite her best efforts, she was unable to gain admission to any of the universities she applied to.

What started as a winter job at Pizza Hut became the first chapter of Jiyoung's long journey through part-time work. From 1995 to 2000, she spent over five years juggling multiple jobs, earning money to fund her studies while working toward her dreams.

Taking Another Shot at College Admissions

Jiyoung was far from an academic underachiever. Her consistently strong grades made college seem like a natural next step. However, the path to higher education turned out to be more challenging than she had anticipated. She had always envisioned herself as a university student, aspiring to become a teacher, but the college entrance exams became an unexpected battleground.

She had never imagined a future without college. After the disappointment of her first attempt, she found herself lost and uncertain about her career path. However, determined to try again, she set her sights on a second attempt. But just as she was preparing, her father's bankruptcy turned her world upside down. The financial strain and daily challenges made studying nearly impossible. Despite her continued efforts, her second attempt ended in disappointment as well.

Jiyoung decided to give the entrance exam one more shot. When she retook the exam, she studied independently at home without attending an academy. However, for her third attempt, she chose to enroll in an academy. Her parents remained neutral, neither strongly encouraging nor discouraging her decision. She developed a grueling routine: working during the day and attending night classes, determined to improve her chances. Despite her hard work and dedication, she faced the disappointment of failing for the third time.

Refusing to give up, Jiyoung prepared for a fourth attempt with a new strategy. Recognizing that post-work study left her too exhausted to focus effectively, she modified her approach. From February to June, she worked intensively to save money, then dedicated herself fully to studying from July to November (the month of Korea's college entrance exam). Despite this meticulous planning, her fourth attempt also resulted in failure.

Jiyoung aspired to attend a college of education or a four-year university in Seoul. Yet, despite her persistent efforts, her scores always fell just short. After three years of relentless dedication, Jiyoung made the difficult and heart-wrenching decision to let go of her college dreams

A Patchwork of Part-Time Jobs

While studying, Jiyoung was responsible for funding all aspects of her life—from basic living expenses like food, transportation, and communication, to study materials such as textbooks, academy fees, and application costs. To make ends meet, she relied heavily on local flea market job boards as her primary source of employment. Her jobs were typically short-term, ranging from one to six months at various establishments. Throughout this period, Jiyoung continually sought out part-time work, often juggling multiple jobs to support herself.

Jiyoung worked as a kitchen assistant at a bar, drawn by the decent pay.

She also took on a part-time flyer distribution job, enticed by the promise of 50,000 won per day. Her task was to go into each building and distribute flyers, often sneaking past security guards trying to prevent her from completing her route. After several confrontations and reprimands, she was ultimately forced to quit.

Jiyoung also endured two grueling months as a telemarketer, working for what she called the "Husband and Wife Scam Team"—a small operation selling insurance over the phone. The job was relentless, with constant pressure, endless rejections, and frequent scoldings. The final straw came when the owners refused to pay her second month's salary. Frustrated and unpaid, she quit.

Jiyoung worked as a bookkeeper at a wholesaler in Sindang-dong, a position she found through the flea market job board. The job required bookkeeping skills and proficiency in abacus calculations, neither of which she had. However, the monthly salary of 700,000 won for a five-day workweek enticed her to apply. The owner, initially seeking a vocational high school graduate, took a chance on Jiyoung. He patiently guided her through the basics of accounting, but her general high school education made it difficult for her to grasp the concepts. Managing large sums of money was overwhelming, and the constant fear of making costly mistakes weighed heavily on her. Eventually, she resigned, feeling she had become more of a burden.

She was too young, with no skills, yet she pushed through—surviving one hustle at a time.

Part-time Work is Also Work

Jiyoung worked as a server at a restaurant in Gwanghwamun. The job fluctuated between quiet lulls and overwhelming rushes, often leaving her to manage the entire restaurant on her own. Concerned about the workload, she approached her boss about hiring additional part-time staff, but he claimed he couldn't afford it and promised that his wife would help out instead. That promise, however, was never fulfilled. When Jiyoung pressed the issue again, her boss fired her on the spot—without paying her for the last month of work.

This incident marked a pivotal shift in her outlook. Until then, Jiyoung had primarily identified as a student, viewing part-time jobs merely as a means to finance her private academy fees. However, after this experience, her perspective on work shifted. She resolved that henceforth, she would leave positions on her own terms—never again be forced out.

Following the restaurant incident, Jiyoung secured a position at a coffee shop. Despite the demanding nature of the work—including being asked to clean floors with a hand mop—she embraced every task. *"I gave my absolute best,"* she recalled, *"motivated by the memory of being unjustly treated at my previous job."* Her dedication did not go unnoticed. When she returned to the coffee shop as a customer, the owner approached her with an offer to raise her hourly wage by 500 won, admitting, *"Other part-time workers quit after just a day or two,"* acknowledging her exceptional commitment.

The Department Store Crucible

Of all her part-time jobs, working in a department store was the longest and most consistent.

> *"Working in a department store was brutal on my legs," Jiyoung recalled. "I'd come home and collapse without even eating dinner."*

Her workdays stretched from 9:00 AM to 8:00 PM, requiring her to stand the entire time in high heels. The exhaustion was relentless, and the pain in her legs never let up. However, the pay was better than most other jobs—30,000 won per day. Working 20 days a month meant she could earn 600,000 won; a full month of work brought in 900,000 won.

Initially, Jiyoung worked at the department store for two months to save money for the application fee when retaking her exam. Later, from February to July, she returned to the store to save up for her fourth exam. After six months of grueling work, she had saved 3 million won, which she used to fund her exam preparations.

Why Didn't Jiyoung Get into College?

In 1995, approximately 800,000 students, including repeat test-takers, sat for the College Scholastic Ability Test (CSAT). This year, the total number of available university admissions—including four-year universities and community colleges—was around 500,000. Seoul's universities, which offered 150,000 spots, required a minimum CSAT score of 115 for admission. A score of 115 or higher granted access to a four-year university in Seoul, while a score of 100 was sufficient for admission to other four-year universities. Those scoring around 80 could enroll in community colleges, as the total number of university spots was roughly 500,000.

— Kim Sunjoo, A Society Divided by 150 Points, Hankyoreh, January 10, 1996.

When Jiyoung was preparing for university, our family was grappling with severe financial hardship. According to Moon Hyejin et al. (2015), a family's socioeconomic background—including parental income and education—plays a crucial role in a student's academic performance and college enrollment. At the time, no one in our family had a stable job or reliable income. Debt collectors regularly showed up at our door, forcing us to relocate frequently.

While preparing for university, Jiyoung had to earn her own money for living expenses and school fees. She spent half of each day working just to make ends meet and the other half attempting to study. However, the relentless cycle left her with little time or energy for proper learning. Exhausted from physically demanding part-time jobs, she struggled to stay focused in her evening academy classes, fighting off fatigue as she pushed through her lessons. Her desperate approach—working for six months to afford six months of study—only underscored the harsh reality of her impossible situation.

"It's Best Not to Change"

Jiyoung took the CSAT four times between 1995 and 1999, a period marked by significant changes in the college entrance examination system.

The CSAT was first introduced in 1993, when she was a high school freshman. Revisions to the national college entrance exam affected not only test-takers that year but also all junior and senior high school students. From 1994 to 1996, universities gained autonomy in determining the weight and composition of CSAT scores, high school grades, and university-specific exams.

The first CSAT comprised 190 questions, scored out of 200, and was divided into four sections: Korean, Mathematics & Inquiry (I), Mathematics & Inquiry (II), and Foreign Language (English). By 1995, when Jiyoung first took the exam, the test had been restructured to separate students into

Humanities, Science, and Arts & Physical Education tracks, better aligning with their respective fields. In 1996, when she retook the exam, the foreign language section saw an increase in listening comprehension questions from none to ten. By 1997, when she attempted the test for the third time, the scoring system changed, doubling the perfect score from 200 to 400 points.

Each year, she had to adjust her study methods and admissions strategy to keep up with the ever-changing requirements. Yet, with no guidance or support, she had to navigate these challenges entirely on her own.

When poverty drains both time and mental capacity, academic achievement becomes an uphill battle. Jiyoung's struggle to enter college wasn't just a personal failure—it was a reflection of a system where success requires more than intelligence and effort; it demands resources many simply don't have.

For Jiyoung, college was more than just an education—it was a dream and a way out of poverty. But she never found her escape.

¶ The year after Jiyoung let go of her college dreams, I became the university student she had once aspired to be. Unlike her constant struggle to balance work and study, my world as a high school student revolved entirely around academics. I had the luxury of dedicating all my time and mental energy to studying, unburdened by the bone-deep exhaustion of physical labor. More importantly, I had the privilege of existing within a structured environment—a school that truly nurtured me. My teachers did more than simply transfer knowledge; they provided crucial guidance, actively shaping my future and dreams within the safety of the classroom walls.

The fundamental difference between Jiyoung and me never lay in our abilities or potential, but in the profound privilege of dedicated time and institutional support. I became what she had desperately yearned to be, not because I possessed greater merit or determination, but simply because I had been granted greater fortune.

Path to Employment

Jiyoung gave up on her college dreams after four attempts, but finding a job proved to be just as difficult.

Struggle After the IMF Crisis

When Jiyoung finally gave up on her college dream, she faced an equally unforgiving reality. Graduating from a general high school—not a vocational one—left her without specialized skills or training. Research by Shin and Oh (2014) underscored the challenge: 40% of female graduates from general high schools, lacking vocational training, struggled with significant employment disadvantages. Jiyoung's situation was a textbook example—she was female, lacked vocational skills, and her only work experience had come from the part-time jobs that consumed her college preparation years.

The timing couldn't have been worse. In 1999, the economic crisis had devastated the job market, driving unemployment to a historic peak of 6.0% in the third quarter—a record that still stands today.

Following the 1997 Asian financial crisis, the Kim Daejung government focused on the IT industry as a key driver of economic recovery. By positioning IT as the engine for national growth, the administration implemented policies to build a digital economy. Recognizing that computer skills could offer new opportunities, Jiyoung understood that acquiring them was crucial for securing a stable job. However, the immediate pressure to earn a living left her with little room for education. The same cycle that had hindered her college aspirations resurfaced—forced to prioritize survival over learning, she found herself once again working at a department store, a convenience store, and similar jobs, trapped in the same predicament.

The First Step Toward Stability

A survey by the Korea Employment Information Center, which analyzed 6,895 young workers who entered their first job between 2007 and 2019, revealed a stark reality. On average, young job seekers spent nineteen months securing their first full-time position. However, for those with only a high school diploma, the wait was even longer—stretching to thirty-five months. For Jiyoung, it took two years of preparation before she finally found stable employment.

During this time, she followed an exhausting routine: juggling part-time jobs, attending computer classes, and endlessly scanning job listings. Most openings were for telemarketing positions—a field she knew all too well, along with its potential pitfalls. But then, she came across a job posting from KT, a public corporation, seeking 114 telephone information operators. Trusting in its established reputation, Jiyoung decided to apply.

Her resume passed the initial screening, and she went through interviews and written tests. In the winter of 2000, she secured the position at KT. While the job was temporary, it carried the credibility of a well-known company—marking her first real step toward stable employment.

Information Telephone Operator

The 114 guidebook included a map of Seoul and instructions for using the computer terminal. 114 telephone operators were required to memorize the entire city map. A key aspect of the receptionist training was pronunciation practice and the memorization of greeting phrases. Operators followed 23 manuals, each designed for different scenarios. For example, the first standard response was as follows:

- *"Hello, customer!"*
- *"Yes, You mean Cheil Academy in Sungin-dong?"*
- *"Yes, I'll be happy to guide you through the process."*

The instructor emphasized that the tone corresponding to "yes" should reflect the warm and friendly quality of the Sol note in the solfège scale. Additionally, the training focused on a speech style where operators ended sentences with the "Da / Na / Ka" pattern, rather than the soft "Yo" commonly heard in daily conversations among 114 receptionists.

Kim Sunmi, 114 Voices of the World I Met as a 114 Telephone Operator, DongA Ilbo, June 12, 2003.

Jiyoung became a 114 telephone operator, responsible for providing callers with the phone numbers of businesses they requested.

Her days quickly settled into a mechanical rhythm. She sat at her terminal, connecting callers to the numbers they needed while meeting daily quotas for answered calls. The work was relentless, shifting between three rotations: Jiyoung alternated between morning and day shifts, while home-based operators covered the night hours.

Her pay was 700,000 won during the three-month probation period, increasing to 1 million won afterward. While her base salary matched that of permanent staff, the benefits stopped there. As a contractor, Jiyoung watched as holidays and bonus seasons came and went, never receiving the extra envelopes that eased her colleagues' lives.

Nightmare Customer

"Calls on rainy days, with phrases like 'I want to kill myself' and obscene remarks, were regular occurrences. There were men moaning while counting from 1 to 10, asking about the color of

Call center work represents a quintessential form of emotional labor. In their 2013 study, *Emotional Labor of Product Salespersons and Telephone Counselors*, Park et al. note that customers in service industries, such as retail and call centers, expect workers to always be "nice" and to suppress their emotions. Failing to meet these expectations can gradually erode a company's reputation and performance. In response, businesses enforce strict control over employees' facial expressions, speech, and behavior, ensuring they align with customer expectations. This is achieved through detailed handbooks outlining behavioral guidelines, constant monitoring of compliance, and pressure to internalize company norms.

Yet in Korea around the year 2000, this systematic commodification of human emotion had yet to be widely recognized as *emotional labor*. Workers were left to endure the strain without acknowledgment or support.

Jiyoung's telephone operator manual was clear: she was required to be polite to every caller, no matter how rude or abusive, and under no circumstances could she hang up first. Each evening, she would come home and recount the worst interaction of the day. The emotional toll of these encounters stayed with her, sometimes driving her to leave work early, tears streaming down her face.

Still, despite the hardships, she held onto her identity as a KT employee. "It's nice to be able to say 'KT' when someone asks me, 'Where do you work?'" she would say.

Privatization and Workforce Restructuring

Following the IMF Crisis, KT underwent aggressive privatization, implementing sweeping organizational consolidation and workforce restructuring. In June 2001, the company severed its 114 directory service, transferring operations to the newly established Korea Post Service. My sister, once proud of her KT affiliation, suddenly found herself reassigned to Korean Info Service.

Officials framed this transition with the sanitized phrase "management rationalization of public enterprises." But in the language of corporate restructuring, "rationalization" often meant downsizing, and "efficiency" translated into job cuts. Behind this bureaucratic jargon, the merger of telephone and internet services created a cutthroat work environment. Some operators were hastily reassigned to unfamiliar online roles, while countless others simply disappeared as their positions were eliminated under the calculated banner of efficiency.

For supervisors, the situation was even harsher. These women, mostly in their fifties and sixties, had spent decades managing teams of fifty operators each, earning full salaries and benefits. Then came the ultimatum: accept a severance package and leave, or stay on as contractors with half the pay. Many chose to stay, their earlier sacrifices—putting family life aside for career advancement—leaving them with few other options. The supervisors, like the 114 telephone operators, were all women. Corporate restructuring never explicitly addressed gender, yet its impact was unmistakable—job cuts, salary reductions, and instability disproportionately affected women, exposing an unspoken but undeniable gender disparity.

A Rare Opportunity

The company incentivized restructuring by offering stock options to full-time employees and a potential path to permanent employment for contract workers who met specific conditions. It was a calculated move—a "carrot" designed to encourage workforce consolidation while easing resistance to restructuring.

Jiyoung seized this opportunity, viewing it as a chance to secure stability and a lasting place within the company.

Each year, the company conducted evaluations, selecting contract employees who had met the required tenure and performance criteria. Assessments were based on metrics such as call volume and customer satisfaction scores. Age also factored into the selection, with older employees often excluded from consideration. Many of Jiyoung's colleagues never made it past this initial screening.

The final selection process was rigorous, consisting of multiple stages: a general knowledge written examination, a formal interview, and a practical service evaluation assessing customer interaction skills. During this period, candidates exchanged rice cakes for good luck—a small tradition amid the pressure.

Jiyoung successfully navigated each stage, officially securing her full-time position in 2002.

However, the program was short-lived. Just one year after Jiyoung transitioned to full-time status, the company eliminated the contract-to-permanent employment pathway entirely, closing the door for future contract workers hoping to follow the same path.

Marriage and a New Chapter

Jiyoung left her position in 2005, a year after getting married.

"Once you become a full-time employee at KT, there's little incentive to leave," Jiyoung explained. "The

Unlike many of her colleagues at the 114 directory service, where all operators were women and many continued working after marriage, Jiyoung found the balance increasingly difficult. "Looking back, I do have some regrets about leaving," she reflected. "But at the time, I was overwhelmed. Balancing work with housework, plus visiting my Mom in the hospital—I would break down crying. If I continued to work, it would have been hard to have children."

After leaving KT, Jiyoung took a two-month break to focus on domestic responsibilities. She then found part-time work at a convenience store near her home, contributing to the household expenses. She continued working there until late in her pregnancy, nearly a full year.

Since then, Jiyoung has dedicated herself to raising her children as a full-time homemaker.

A Vanishing Opportunity: Can Another Jiyoung Succeed Today?

In 2002, Lee Hyosoo analyzed labor market dynamics through the framework of dual labor market theory, which categorizes employment into two distinct segments: the primary and secondary markets. The primary labor market is associated with quality employment, offering strong job security and stability, consistent wage growth, clear career advancement pathways, advanced technological infrastructure, professional management practices, and robust union representation. In contrast, the secondary labor market is characterized by employment instability, high turnover, low and stagnant wages, limited or nonexistent advancement opportunities, and simple, repetitive tasks that require minimal training.

A key feature of this system is the limited mobility between these two markets. The structural division tends to perpetuate, and even worsen, the disparities between them. Workers who spend significant time in the secondary labor market often find themselves unable to meet the entry requirements for the primary market, effectively blocking their access to better opportunities. This entrenchment in the secondary market further widens the gap between the two segments.

Jiyoung's story is remarkable within this framework. As a high school graduate without specialized skills, she entered the workforce during one of South Korea's most challenging economic periods - the aftermath of the IMF crisis. This era was marked by widespread corporate bankruptcies, extensive restructuring, and record-high unemployment rates. The push for labor market flexibility had led to a surge in temporary and contract positions, and Jiyoung initially joined KT as a contractor.

Her career trajectory - progressing from part-time to contract work, and ultimately to full-time employment at a major corporation - represents a notable success story of upward mobility. She displayed remarkable determination in seeking better opportunities, focusing on both academic and professional growth. However, her journey prompts a crucial question: Could someone replicate her success in today's labor market?

In 1995, when Jiyoung took her college entrance exam, South Korea's higher education enrollment rate stood at 54.1%. This figure had skyrocketed from 23.7% in 1980 to 68% in 2000, peaking at over 80% before settling in the 70% range in recent years. Despite this surge in university graduates, securing stable employment has become increasingly difficult, making opportunities for high school graduates even more scarce.

The employment landscape has fundamentally changed since 2000, shaped by persistent economic slowdown and jobless growth. Two concerning trends have emerged and become entrenched: the rise of low-wage, precarious employment, and a deepening divide in the dual labor market - both between large and small companies, and between regular and non-regular employees.

The shift in industrial structure driven by the development of new technologies, such as the rise of the internet and smartphones, has contributed to growing unemployment. In Jiyoung's field, the transformation has been particularly dramatic. Between 2002 and 2020, the annual call volume for directory services dropped to just one-tenth of its previous level. This sharp decline in demand was mirrored by a significant reduction in the workforce, with the number of 114 operators shrinking from 4,000 to just 691.

Jiyoung was among the last to benefit from the contract-to-permanent employment pathway. After her transition to full-time status, the company discontinued this advancement opportunity. Her successors remained perpetually in contract positions, regardless of their performance metrics or customer service excellence.

§ *Jiyoung is someone who prioritizes others over herself. Amid the uncertainty of repeated college entrance exam failures and an unclear future, she consistently placed her family's needs above her own. She took on the burden of her father's debts, supported her nephews' childcare expenses, and remained a steady support for her mother. Yet, her own life was equally unstable, with ongoing academic setbacks and an uncertain future.*

Despite her own challenges, Jiyoung's support for me never faltered. She prepared my daily lunches during my study and believed in my potential even when I struggled to find a job after graduation. Her unwavering faith and support, given her own difficult circumstances, were constant.

I carry a profound debt of gratitude that I feel I can never fully repay.

In everyday use, "Ganan" (meaning *poverty*) and "Bingon" (meaning *destitution*) may seem synonymous, but subtle differences exist between the two. "Ganan" is derived from the term "Gannan" (艱難), which combines two characters: Gan (艱), meaning "difficulty," and Nan (難), meaning "hardship." From this, the word Ganan (家難) is formed—combining Ga (家), meaning "house," and Nan (難), meaning "difficulty"—which is associated with disaster and ruin within the household.

(...)

Poverty is not a simple condition—it is a phenomenon shaped and sustained by multiple surrounding structures. I would argue that what often appears as personal or familial misfortune is, in reality, the result of inevitable or arbitrary systemic forces. Within this framework, a certain path—a pattern—has already been laid out.

— So Juncheol, *The Grammar of Poverty*

Chapter 3: Yoojung Kang

A Single Mother's Journey: From Struggle to Independence

Yoojung, my oldest sister, once dreamed of a "normal" life—finding a loving partner, building a family, and nurturing a home. But at 29, that dream was shattered when she became the sole provider for her two young children, then just three and five years old. She searched for jobs that fit within the constraints of daycare, kindergarten, and school hours, taking whatever work she could find—whether in homestyle Chinese, Japanese, and Korean restaurants, a kimbap shop, or a supermarket. Despite her relentless efforts, earning only minimum wage made it nearly impossible to make ends meet, and she had to rely on financial support from our family.

As her children entered middle and high school, Yoojung found a new opportunity as a truck courier driver. Unlike her previous jobs, her earnings were no longer limited to the minimum hourly wage but instead reflected her skills and effort. This change empowered her to support her children independently, without needing family assistance. Today, she continues to work as a truck courier driver, and the children who were once so young are now adults.

Profile

- Name : Yoojung Kang
- Birth Year : 1975
- Education : Vocational High School Graduate
- Work Experience : 24 years (excluding 8 years of career breaks)
- Started Working At : 18 years old
- Occupation History : Bookkeeper, restaurant staff (kimbap, Chinese, Japanese, Korean cuisine, etc.), supermarket cashier & sales associate, truck courier driver, etc.

After High School

During the summer vacation of her sophomore year in vocational high school, Yoojung took her first part-time job at Lotteria, a fast-food chain, alongside a friend. It wasn't out of financial necessity but rather curiosity—she wanted to experience the part-time jobs that many of her peers were taking.

The job was neither hard nor demanding. Each month, employees were assigned specific products to promote, often featuring new menu items. Yoojung had a natural talent for sales— during her shifts, the burgers she recommended consistently became bestsellers, earning her the nickname "Queen of Suggestions." Though her success didn't come with monetary rewards, it gave her a strong sense of pride and accomplishment.

As summer ended, Yoojung attempted to continue working by switching to afternoon shifts. However, this meant returning home around 11 PM. Concerned about her safety on late-night commutes, my Dad insisted she quit, and she eventually stopped working at Lotteria.

Starting a Career in Small Business

During the second semester of her senior year at high school, Yoojung secured a job as a bookkeeper at a small business on the recommendation of her homeroom teacher. The company was owned by a friend of her teacher.

At the time, Yoojung lacked clear career direction. As her second semester progressed, she watched her classmates secure employment or prepare for recruitment exams, often missing classes for interviews. The growing number of empty desks in her classroom diminished her motivation to attend school.

"In those days, most students remained at their internship placements during their senior year,"

The company Yoojung joined manufactured and sold uninterruptible power supply (UPS) systems. It operated from two separate facilities: an office and a factory. The office staff consisted of just three people—the president, the general manager, and Yoojung—while the factory employed four to five production workers. The company was in an expansion phase, with the president overseeing the construction of an additional manufacturing facility near Seoul.

Yoojung handled a range of administrative tasks, primarily bookkeeping and bank transactions. After completing her three-month probationary period, she was promoted to full-time status.

Transition to Corporate Life

In 1994, Yoojung secured a position at a major pharmaceutical company through her father's connections. While she followed her father's guidance in taking the position, he didn't fully grasp the prestige of working for a large corporation at the time. Her father's motivation wasn't focused on her career development or professional success—he simply hoped she would meet a suitable marriage prospect within the company.

Assigned to the sales support team as a junior bookkeeper, Yoojung's responsibilities included processing orders from hospitals and pharmacies, as well as routine office tasks like preparing coffee, making photocopies, and retrieving documents from the archives.

Her official work hours were from 8 a.m. to 6 p.m., but she often worked significant overtime. Despite the demanding schedule, her compensation package was substantial: a base salary of 600,000 won with a 600% bonus. At the time, male university graduates earned an average monthly salary of 650,000 won. Though she had only completed high school, her position at a large corporation allowed her to earn wages comparable to those of male graduates from four-year universities.

The company maintained a strict hierarchy based on educational background. Each team followed a five-tier structure: general manager, deputy general manager, assistant manager, senior bookkeeper, and junior bookkeeper. General managers and deputy general managers held four-year university degrees, assistant managers were community college graduates, and bookkeepers were typically selected from prestigious vocational high schools. The sales team was exclusively male, mostly composed of Reserve Officer Training Corps (ROTC) graduates.

Despite this rigid structure, the assistant manager often played the most crucial role in day-to-day operations. With 15 to 20 years of experience, they possessed the deepest knowledge of the business. The general manager and deputy general manager, younger and less experienced, relied heavily on the assistant manager's expertise. However, regardless of their competence, assistant managers were rarely promoted due to their academic credentials.

"Bookkeepers were often showered with gifts from the sales staff," Yoojung recalled. *"Office romances between bookkeepers and salespeople were common, and many led to marriage."*

The company employed many women and actively encouraged female engagement through initiatives like volunteer work. However, married women were noticeably absent. Though there was no official policy against it, an unspoken expectation dictated that women resign upon marriage. Yoojung recalled only one exception—a woman who had served the company for over a decade. Despite facing significant pressure to quit after her marriage, she remained steadfast in her refusal to leave.

In 1995, Yoojung married a production worker she had met at her first company. In line with the prevailing social norms, she resigned from her job upon marriage.

Three Friends, Three Journeys

Yoojung's closest friends—Misun, Hyejin, and Jisun—graduated in February 1994 and all secured positions at Company A, a major food corporation in Sinseol-dong.

As sales representatives, their work involved traveling to supermarkets, public fairs, and various promotional events to showcase and sell company products. The job was demanding, made even more challenging by Company A's intense corporate culture, which included "mental training" sessions filled with motivational chants like *"You can do it!"* These high-energy drills often left them emotionally exhausted.

Their career paths took an unexpected turn during the 1997 Asian Financial Crisis. Facing economic turmoil, Company A restructured its workforce, converting full-time employees— including the three friends—into contract workers.

Misun, known for her unwavering loyalty, remained with Company A despite the demotion. True to her nature, she stayed until her marriage at age 28, having dedicated nearly a decade to the company.

Hyejin and Jisun, however, chose a different path. They transitioned to Company B, a major corporation expanding into distribution, taking on roles similar to those they held at Company A. Hyejin worked there for three years before leaving upon her marriage.

Jisun, on the other hand, thrived in sales. At Company A, she consistently ranked No. 1 at every store she worked in, securing prime shelf placements for her products—expanding from a single space to five. Her success didn't come easily; she engaged in daily battles with competing promotional staff, yet she always emerged victorious, earning a near-legendary reputation in the industry.

At Company B, her dominance continued. She remained the top sales performer across all supermarket locations, catching the attention of upper management. Impressed by her results, Company B recruited her into its corporate marketing team at headquarters.

However, corporate life was an entirely different challenge. As the only team member without a college degree, Jisun struggled with unfamiliar tasks like computer work and formal presentations. The aggressive confidence that had propelled her in the field felt out of place in the boardroom. In her sales days, she had no hesitation in physically confronting male competitors who encroached on her territory—but now, she was navigating a world where success relied on paperwork and strategy rather than direct competition.

After a year at headquarters, Jisun decided to forge her own path. Through a relative's introduction, she entered the clothing distribution business, sourcing products from wholesalers and selling to retailers. Sometimes, she reflects, *"If I had pursued night school back then, things might have been different,"* but her sharp business instincts have led her to impressive success. Today, she has expanded her retail operations beyond Korea, tapping into the Chinese market.

A Single Mother's Struggle

Yoojung had once dreamed of a conventional life, where she could raise her children with her husband's financial support. However, that dream never materialized. In 2003, at just 29 years old, she became the sole provider for her two young children, ages 3 and 5.

Troubles Never Come Alone

With only a high school diploma and an eight-year gap in her employment history due to marriage and childcare, Yoojung faced limited job prospects. As she approached 30, she realized that returning to her previous bookkeeping job was no longer feasible. Even if she could, balancing full-time work while raising two small children alone seemed impossible.

She first took a night shift at a cell phone assembly plant, so she could care for her children during the day. Every evening, she would leave them with her family and head to work. However, her young children, missing their mother, would wake up during the night searching for her and often fell ill with colds and fevers. After just two months, the situation became unsustainable, and Yoojung was forced to quit.

Yoojung found it incredibly difficult to raise her two young children while working full-time. She sought part-time jobs that aligned with daycare hours. However, these roles paid barely above minimum wage, limiting her work to four to six hours a day. On part-time wages alone, it was financially impossible for Yoojung to adequately support her children or provide them with the life they deserved.

Yoojung's extended family (our family) wanted to help, but their own financial struggles limited their support. Her father worked as a motorcycle courier driver, struggling to support the family while paying off debts from a previous business failure. Her mother worked as a cleaner but couldn't provide childcare. I was a college student, unable to contribute much. Her other sister, Jiyoung, who had stable employment, covered the daycare expenses for a while, but after her marriage, she could no longer continue.

Then, an even greater hardship struck. Our Mom suffered a brain hemorrhage at work. The stroke left her paralyzed on her right side, severely impaired her mobility, and robbed her of the ability to speak. She required round-the-clock care in the hospital.

The Korea Urban Institute (2004) notes that when a working-age household member becomes disabled or seriously ill, the resulting loss of labor capacity often leads to material deprivation. In low-income families, illness not only reduces income but also increases essential expenses, worsening financial instability.

My family made a pragmatic economic decision. Hiring a professional caregiver would have cost approximately 2,500,000 won monthly—more than anyone in the family earned. Having a family member provide care made more sense both financially and emotionally for our Mom.

We carefully evaluated who could shoulder this responsibility: my Dad, burdened with outstanding debts; my sister Yoojung, focused on raising two young children; Jiyoung, recently married and providing the family's only stable income; and me, a recent college graduate preparing to enter the workforce who seemed the logical choice.

However, concerned about derailing her 24-year-old sibling's future prospects, Jiyoung made a significant sacrifice. She paid off the remainder of my Dad's debts, enabling him to leave his motorcycle courier job and become Mom's full-time caregiver at the hospital.

This crisis forced us to reorganize our family's resources. Yoojung moved into our parents' now-empty house, eliminating her rental expenses. Since my Mom's injury qualified as an industrial accident, insurance covered the hospital bills and some caregiving expenses. My Dad shared a portion of the monthly care allowance he received with Yoojung, supplementing her income from part-time work during her children's kindergarten hours.

Each of us making sacrifices to protect one another in our most difficult times.

A Life Below the Poverty Line

In 2007, after three years in the hospital, my parents returned home. My Mom still required round-the-clock care.

Once again, our family faced a difficult decision. If my Dad resumed work as a motorcycle courier, he could earn around 2 million won per month. In contrast, Yoojung, even with full-time employment, would make only 600,000–700,000 won, and her children were still young and needed care. After careful consideration, we decided that my Dad would return to work, while Yoojung would take on household responsibilities and care for our Mom.

To support the household, my Dad provided Yoojung with 1.2 million won per month for living expenses. She supplemented this by working part-time, earning an additional 300,000–400,000 won.

From 2007 to 2015, five people—Yoojung, our parents, and her two school-aged children—lived together in a cramped, aging 13-pyeong (approximately 430-square-foot) rowhouse. With only two bedrooms, the living room was repurposed as an additional sleeping space.

During this period, the government-set minimum living wage for a family of five averaged around 1.7 million won per month. Yet, Yoojung's household survived on just 1.5–1.6 million won, falling below the threshold for basic living expenses.

Though our family managed to meet our most basic needs for food and shelter, our living conditions remained substandard, and daily life presented constant challenges. The situation took its toll on everyone—Yoojung struggled, her children grew up in difficult conditions, and the entire family endured twelve long years of relentless adversity.

Twelve Years of Hustle: Restaurants, Grocery Stores, and More

Yoojung worked while her children were in kindergarten or school, adjusting her schedule as they grew. Though her work hours shifted to align with their schooling, the nature of her jobs remained largely the same—she earned a living primarily through restaurant and grocery store work. To supplement her income, she also took on temporary roles, including election administration and promotional event jobs.

Her most reliable employer was a kimbap restaurant near her home. Here, Yoojung's role extended far beyond making kimbap rolls—she served customers, managed the cash register, cleaned the establishment, and washed dishes. Her shifts covered the busy morning commute hours and the hectic lunch period.

She also worked as a lunchtime server at a Japanese restaurant from 10 AM to 3 PM. She assisted in the kitchen of a steamed seafood restaurant, and, once her children were old enough to manage without her for short periods, took evening shifts at a Chinese restaurant.

Yoojung's employment history also included retail positions. She worked as a yogurt sales representative at a large supermarket and as a cashier at a local grocery store.

The most demanding job Yoojung held was at a well-known *Baekban* restaurant (a Korean homestyle eatery) in Daeheung-dong, renowned for its lunch service. Their signature dish was grilled fish served with a variety of traditional side dishes. Her workday began at 10 AM, preparing and frying fish while making numerous banchan (side dishes). By noon, she was serving a steady stream of customers, and once the lunch rush died down, she cleaned up—often not finishing until 3 PM.

This job offered the highest pay she had ever earned—10,000 won per hour, plus a daily serving of what the staff jokingly called "expensive" yogurt. Despite her remarkable physical endurance—she had never been hospitalized and rarely even caught a cold—the relentless demands of the job proved too much. Even with the higher wages, she could only manage for three months.

Yoojung typically stayed at each establishment for six months to a year, sometimes leaving when temporary contracts ended. Most of her employers were small businesses with little financial stability. She often had to quit when part-time positions were no longer available or when the business itself struggled. In some cases, she lost jobs due to store closures or bankruptcies. Each time she left a job, she quickly found another—usually within a week.

She worked like that for 12 years—those were the challenging years.

The Structural Challenges of a Single Mother's Poverty

When a spouse can no longer provide financially—whether due to divorce, bereavement, or other circumstances—women are often forced into precarious, low-wage jobs. This structural disadvantage plays a central role in the feminization of poverty.

As Kim Anna (2006) discusses in *Women's Poverty and Poverty Measures in Korean Society*, published in *Health and Social Research*, women striving for economic stability face overwhelming barriers, particularly the lack of accessible social support services. High childcare costs, the mismatch between childcare availability and work schedules, and the scarcity of after-school programs severely limit employment opportunities. Women carry the dual responsibility of wage labor and caregiving, while female heads of households face even greater challenges, juggling the roles of breadwinner, primary caregiver, and domestic worker simultaneously.

Our family wanted Yoojung to find full-time employment, but this suggestion ignored a crucial question: Could she realistically raise two young children on her own while working full-time? My Mom also encouraged her to learn a trade, such as hairdressing, but Yoojung couldn't afford the tuition. More urgently, she needed both income and time to care for her children.

Yoojung faced multiple barriers in the labor market—her limited high school education, gender, age, and the significant gap in her employment history. Finding stable work proved exceptionally difficult. Even when she secured positions, circumstances consistently undermined her efforts, as demonstrated by her brief experience as a night-shift factory worker, which she abandoned after two months when her children fell ill. With her children just 3 and 5 years old and no reliable childcare support, her options remained severely limited.

The harsh mathematics of Yoojung's situation made full-time employment an impractical solution. Jobs available to her typically paid around 700,000 won monthly, while the minimum living costs for a family of three at that time ranged from 800,000 to 900,000 won. Beyond housing, food, and healthcare expenses, full-time work would require full-day childcare for both children—an additional financial burden. Even working full-time, she would struggle to reach the minimum subsistence level.

The fundamental reality was that Yoojung could not possibly support two children entirely on her own. Family assistance was not merely helpful—it was essential. Given these constraints, she "chose" the only viable option: caring for her children while working part-time.

Kim Anna's 2006 research, drawing from the 2003 Urban Household Survey, revealed a disturbing pattern: among female heads of households, only 15% secured full-time positions, while 36% worked as temporary or casual laborers. Among those temporary and casual workers, 28.1% lived below the minimum subsistence level, with one in three female-headed households falling below this poverty threshold.

Yoojung's experience was not an anomaly but a representative example of the systemic challenges facing female heads of households.

Truck Courier Driver

As Yoojung's children entered middle and high school, her caregiving responsibilities diminished. However, her financial challenges intensified—expenses were increasing while living space remained cramped in the shared family home.

The time had come for Yoojung to establish independence from her parents' household.

Time for Independence

In 2015, the government-established minimum cost of living for a family of three was 1,359,688 won. With the minimum hourly wage set at 5,580 won, even working a full 8-hour day made it nearly impossible for Yoojung to earn 1 million won per month.

Even if she secured a slightly higher-paying job, her income would barely cover the minimum subsistence level for her family. The minimum living wage represented the barest of necessities—far from an adequate or comfortable standard of living. For context, in 2015, the median cost of living for a family of three was 3,441,364 won. Yoojung simply couldn't support her family on wages alone.

Despite these challenges, Yoojung possessed remarkable qualities that her family recognized. Her hands were quick and nimble, allowing her to clean every corner without leaving a speck of dust and wash clothes to a like-new condition. Her cooking skills were impressive, and she maintained excellent physical stamina while demonstrating quick thinking. Perhaps most importantly, once she committed to a task, she saw it through to the end. She was someone who could create value far beyond the minimum wage.

After carefully evaluating her options and abilities, our family made a pivotal decision: instead of continuing to navigate the constraints of hourly employment, Yoojung would venture into entrepreneurship, even if it meant starting small.

A New Beginning: The Damas Mini-Truck Courier Driver

Our family had 30 million won to invest in starting Yoojung's business.

With her extensive restaurant experience, she initially considered opening a Tteokbokki restaurant, which required relatively modest startup costs. However, her years in small restaurants had given her valuable insight into the challenges of food service management. She recognized that if the Tteokbokki venture failed, she could lose not only her entire investment but also potentially incur additional debt from lease obligations and other expenses.

Drawing on his experience as a motorcycle courier, my Dad suggested an alternative: becoming a truck courier driver. Although uncommon for women, this service, using a

Damas mini-truck, posed fewer physical risks than motorcycle delivery. The startup requirements were simple—purchasing a vehicle and obtaining a business license plate—both of which were within her budget. This option also provided a valuable safety net: even if the business didn't succeed, she could recover 60-70% of her investment by selling the vehicle and license plate. Additionally, business license plates often appreciated over time, offering a potential investment benefit.

Two major obstacles stood in Yoojung's way. First, she didn't have a driver's license—obtaining a Class 1 regular license was a prerequisite for operating a Damas vehicle. Second, her geographic knowledge was extremely limited. For forty years, her movements had been restricted primarily to home and nearby workplaces, leaving her unfamiliar with the broader road network essential for delivery work.

Despite these challenges, our family remained steadfast in our belief in her abilities. I contributed the 30 million won capital, which I had saved over nine years of employment after paying off student loans and housing debts. My Dad leveraged local connections to arrange the purchase of a Damas vehicle and business license plate through a neighborhood courier driver operator. Yoojung focused on obtaining her driver's license, though the process was not easy—she failed the test three times before finally passing on her fourth attempt.

In May 2015, after overcoming these substantial obstacles, Yoojung officially began her new career as a Damas truck courier driver, marking the start of a new chapter in her professional life.

Breaking Gender Barriers

The delivery industry's gender imbalance was stark.

"In my experience, truck courier driving is a male-dominated field," Yoojung observed. *"Younger men in their 40s typically drive high-end*

Na Youngsun's 1998 study, *The Status of Women's Vocational Training and the Development of Promising Occupations*, highlighted this disparity through quantitative analysis. Using 30% and 70% thresholds—where professions with 70% or more women were considered "traditionally female," those with 30-70% women "mixed," and those with less than 30% women "non-traditional" for women—Na uncovered a revealing pattern. Only eight occupations qualified as traditionally female, including secretarial work and textile manufacturing. In contrast, thirty-four occupations were classified as non-traditional, fields historically inaccessible to women due to masculine stereotyping or women's limited technical education opportunities.

The career paths Na recommended for women in 1998 reflected the narrow vision of female employment at the time. These "promising occupations" mostly clustered around traditionally feminine domains: textile and clothing repair, certified roles like hairdressing and Korean food preparation, childcare positions such as tutoring, and service roles in beauty and health. Even entrepreneurial suggestions emphasized conventionally feminine small businesses like flower shops.

Transportation services—specifically the truck courier driving that Yoojung eventually chose—were conspicuously absent from these recommendations.

This gender-based occupational segregation had profound economic consequences. As Kim Anna (2006) observed: "Due to the polarization of occupations by gender, women are concentrated in low-wage, unskilled labor, and their wages remain about 65% of men's wages. Women are disproportionately employed in blue-collar jobs, services, and office work, while significantly underrepresented in technical and managerial occupations, demonstrating their concentration in low-wage, unskilled positions."

Yoojung's decision to enter the truck courier industry—explicitly outside the realm of traditionally "female" occupations—proved to be a strategically significant move. Had she chosen one of the typically "female" professions, financial independence would likely have remained out of reach, given the systematic undervaluation of work in female-dominated fields. By entering a male-dominated sector, Yoojung positioned herself to earn wages comparable to those of her male counterparts, circumventing some of the structural disadvantages inherent in traditionally female roles.

Rising Strong

When Yoojung first began working as a truck courier driver, she faced several challenges. She was unfamiliar with the roads and often stalled the manual van. As a result, her income was understandably low at first—but this was expected. To prepare for the initial struggle, she kept her part-time restaurant job, working four hours a day to maintain a steady income while dedicating the rest of her time to deliveries and improving her skills.

Soon, Yoojung became familiar with the delivery routes and no longer needed to juggle her part-time job. She developed valuable strategies, such as picking up multiple deliveries at once and targeting areas on the outskirts of Seoul, where traffic was less congested than in the downtown core.

While being a woman in a male-dominated industry presented challenges, she also found that it could work to her advantage. "Some people trust me specifically because I'm a woman," she explains. "I've built relationships with regular customers who may not pay the standard delivery fee but offer me consistent business. It's not a huge financial gain, but it's a steady source of income."

The job fit her well—though admittedly, her options were limited. She enjoyed the independence, with no supervisor constantly watching over her, and loved traveling throughout Seoul and occasionally to provincial areas. After 40 years of being confined to her home and immediate neighborhood, this newfound freedom was exhilarating.

Best of all, she earned money directly proportional to her efforts. In her first two years as a Damas courier driver, she worked enthusiastically from 5 a.m. to 10 p.m., achieving a monthly net income exceeding 4 million won.

When her friends saw her success, they were inspired to start their own delivery services, eventually bringing in three or four others, including a friend, her friend's husband, and some of her friend's relatives. However, Yoojung remains the only one still operating a truck courier business. The others quit after a year or two, struggling with the solitude of the job or feeling dissatisfied with their earnings.

About two years after establishing her delivery service, Yoojung was able to move out of her parents' home and begin a new chapter of her life, taking her two children with her for a fresh, independent start.

Monthly Fixed Costs for Damas Courier Delivery:

- **Gas:** 250,000 won (based on an average of 100,000 km driven annually, with subsidized fuel prices)
- **Repairs:** 200,000 won (for maintenance such as wheels, oil changes, etc.; vehicle replacement every 3-5 years)
- **Shipping Brokerage Platform Usage Fee:** 33,000 won (550 won × 30 days × 2 phones)
- **Hacking Software Fees:** 140,000 won (70,000 won × 2 phones, to help secure orders quickly)
- **Insurance:** 80,000 won (covering driver's and cargo insurance)
- **Other Expenses:** Various parking fees, highway tolls, etc.

This Too Shall Pass

Yoojung continues her work as a truck courier driver to this day, driving over 10 hours a day. Her job involves transporting hundreds of packages, a task known in the industry as "stick work." With no predictable schedule, regular meals are a luxury she can't afford. Instead, she keeps bread, rice cakes, and sweet potatoes in her vehicle to eat on the go.

A truck courier's income is heavily dependent on the economic climate. Yoojung's regular clients were mainly cosmetics and clothing stores in Myeong-dong. However, in 2017, when Chinese tourism dropped sharply due to China's retaliation against South Korea's deployment of the THAAD missile defense system, Myeong-dong merchants reported sales losses exceeding 40%. This resulted in the cancellation of all her regular contracts. Similarly, the COVID-19 pandemic, which began in 2020, brought new challenges. As the economy weakened, not only did her regular deliveries disappear, but the overall work volume dropped, and delivery fees steadily declined year after year.

Despite these setbacks, Yoojung has managed to earn enough to overcome poverty. Her children, who were just 3 and 5 when she started, are now in their twenties. Though the journey was long and difficult, their financial hardship is now behind them.

Understanding the Delivery Fee Structure: What Makes Courier Drivers Earn Less?

The financial structure for truck courier drivers is complex, involving multiple fee arrangements, communication systems, and increasingly competitive pricing.

Courier drivers typically work through local delivery shops, which use delivery service brokerage programs to connect customer orders with available drivers. When a customer places an order at a shop, the shop enters the order into the brokerage program. Yoojung's shop uses Inseong Data, the leading provider of delivery service brokerage software in the industry.

Shops control the visibility of orders in stages. Initially, orders are visible only to drivers within their own network. If these drivers don't accept the order, it becomes visible to all drivers on the platform. This tiered approach gives affiliated drivers first access to more desirable deliveries—those with shorter distances and higher fees. Orders that reach the broader pool tend to be less profitable, with drivers often referring to them as "ridiculously cheap deliveries."

The brokerage system charges a hefty 20% fee on each delivery, which is deducted directly from the driver's payment. Additionally, if a driver accepts an order from a shop they are not affiliated with, the shop earns a 3% commission—also subtracted from the driver's fee.

This system benefits the shops by allowing them to fulfill customer orders without maintaining a large in-house workforce. They focus on customer acquisition and outsource the delivery logistics, earning commissions even when using external drivers.

While drivers technically have the opportunity to increase their earnings by accepting deliveries from multiple shops, the reality is less favorable. Most public orders offer below-market rates, and intense competition among independent drivers continually drives down delivery fees. As self-employed contractors without collective bargaining power, courier drivers have limited leverage to negotiate better terms.

Some delivery shops engage in a practice known as "sharpening," where they quote customers a delivery fee of 30,000 won but report only 20,000 won to the brokerage platform. This allows the shop to pocket a 10,000 won profit margin, while drivers—whether affiliated or independent—are paid based only on the lower reported amount of 20,000 won.

Another significant challenge for courier drivers is the use of hacking software. These applications interface with official brokerage platforms to give drivers earlier access to orders. Although technically illegal, these programs are widely used in the industry. As Yoojung explains, "I don't know a single driver who doesn't use them." Drivers don't use this software to outpace their colleagues, but out of necessity—without it, securing enough orders to make a living would be nearly impossible. Yoojung was first introduced to this "supporter program" by a courier shop owner.

Hacking software providers distribute their programs through text message links, bypassing official platforms like the Google Play Store. Monthly subscription costs range from 50,000 won to 150,000 won, depending on performance capabilities. Yoojung regularly receives messages promoting new versions with "better performance," which causes anxiety and compels her to continually upgrade to more expensive options.

Inseong Data, which dominates 70% of the brokerage platform market, operates through two separate sharing networks. As a result, drivers using Inseong's platform must manage at least two phones to receive orders from both networks. Each phone requires separate installations of both the Inseong brokerage app and the hacking software, essentially doubling their monthly technology costs.

§ Yoojung's favorite phrase is "This too shall pass." It's a comforting reminder during tough times and a humbling one during moments of happiness.

She describes herself as "slow"—slow to grasp concepts in school and slow to realize she needed to carve her own path in life. Yet this deliberate pace has served her well, allowing her to progress steadily, one step at a time, through life's challenges.

Heejung's salary in 2017 was 1.71 million won, and she had expected it to increase the following year in line with the rise in the minimum wage.

(...)

As the minimum wage increased, the basic salary rose, but other salary components were consistently reduced each year. In 2019, the minimum wage was 8,350 won, an increase of 820 won (10.9%) from the previous year. While this should have resulted in a salary increase, Heejung's salary remained the same from 2018 to 2021. As the minimum wage increased, her total salary remained stagnant due to continuous reductions in components other than the basic salary, such as job allowances and incentives. When factoring in the rise in the four major insurance premiums and inflation, her wages were, in reality, declining.

— Nam Bora et al., *Hell of Intermediate Exploitation*

Chapter 4: Minjoon Lee

The Struggles of Student Workers: Balancing Work, Education, and Opportunity

"I'm writing a book and would love to interview you," I explained.

"What's it about?" Minjoon asked.

"Work—labor, jobs," I replied.

"I've only ever worked part-time," he said modestly.

Minjoon, my nephew, stands at 192 centimeters tall. He has always been large for his age, weighing over 10 kilograms by the time he was six months old. His mother often recalls, "I'm sorry I couldn't carry him when he was little," remembering how his size made it impossible to lift him.

Now 22 years old, Minjoon has already accumulated six years of work experience. He started his first part-time job as a restaurant server in his third year of middle school, already towering at 180 centimeters. By 16, he was working 12-hour days. Throughout high school, he made motorcycle food deliveries, rarely taking a day off each month, which often led to tardiness at school. In college, Minjoon continued working part-time. When the bar he worked at shut down due to COVID-19, he quickly found another job at a hotel—without even taking a week off. He stayed at the hotel until just two weeks before enlisting for mandatory military service in October 2021. He is currently serving in the military.

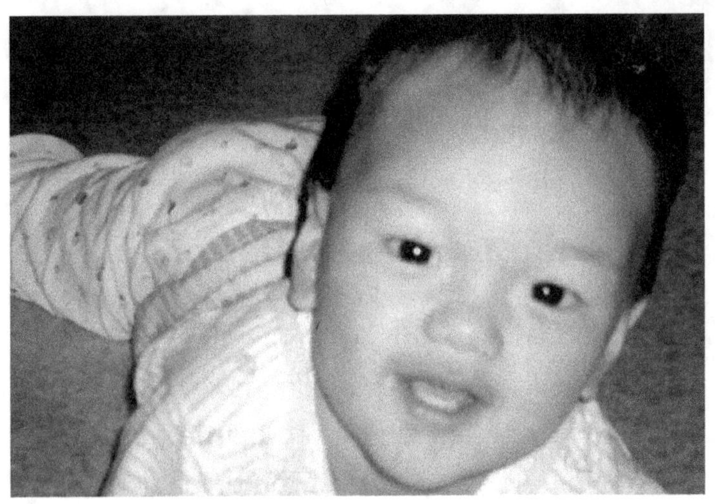

Profile

- Name : Minjoon Lee
- Birth Year : 2001
- Education : Community College (currently on leave for military service)
- Work Experience : 6 years
- Started Working At : 16 years old

- Occupation History : Restaurant/bar staff, food delivery driver, hotel room manager, etc.

Student Workers

Part-Time Job in Middle School

Minjoon began his working life during the winter break of his third year in middle school, taking a part-time job at a pork cutlet restaurant in Hongdae. He got the position through a friend who was already working there. When asked how common part-time jobs were among his peers, Minjoon estimated that only three or four students in his class of 30 to 40 had jobs.

Article 64 of the Labor Standards Act (Minimum Age and Employment License): A person under the age of 15 (or under 18 and still enrolled in middle school under the Elementary and Secondary Education Act) may not be employed as a worker. However, an exception applies to those who hold an Employment Permit Certificate issued by the Minister of

The pork cutlet restaurant was owned by a man in his 60s who rarely visited. His wife, around the same age, was present but mostly remained seated. Her brother managed the kitchen, while Minjoon, despite being just a part-time worker and 16 years old, was solely responsible for all customer service duties. Minjoon worked at the restaurant for eight months, from the winter break of his final year in middle school through the summer break of his first year in high school.

His responsibilities included greeting customers, taking orders, inputting them into the point-of-sale system, preparing rice bowls, and serving completed meals. The kitchen staff would add the pork cutlet and garnishes to the rice he prepared. On an average day, the restaurant generated around 1 million won in sales.

During school vacations, Minjoon worked what amounted to "full-time" hours—10:00 AM to 10:00 PM daily. After starting high school, he reduced his schedule to weekends only, working

10:00 AM to 5:00 PM. When he first started, his hourly wage was 8,500 won, which later increased to 9,000 won. For reference, the minimum wage in 2016 was 6,030 won. He received his pay on a weekly basis.

Article 69 of the Labor Standards Act (Working Hours): The working hours for persons aged 15 to 18 shall not exceed 7 hours per day and 35 hours per week. However, the hours may be extended by agreement between the parties, up to a limit of 1 hour per day and 5 hours per week.

Youth Labor Rights Survey Results (2020)

The National Human Rights Commission conducted a survey from August 18 to October 26, 2020, among youth aged 13 to 24 who had worked within the past year. The findings were published in the *2020 Youth Labor Rights Situation Report*.

1. Age When First Starting Work

Ages 15-18: 54.8%, Ages 18-20: 25.5%, Ages 13-15: 12.4%, Ages 20+: 6.8%

Note: 0.6% started working at age 13, which is prohibited by law

2. Reasons for Working (Multiple Responses)

Personal living expenses: 78.1%, Insufficient pocket money: 48.1%, To gain work/social experience: 31.9%, To help with family expenses: 9.3%, To pay for school fees: 6.1%

3. Job Search Methods (Multiple Responses)

Internet/app job boards: 75.1%, Friends or acquaintances: 62.0%, Adults (family and friends): 14.6%, WorkNet (Online employment service platform provided by the Ministry of Employment and Labor of Korea): 9.9%, Store advertisements: 8.0%, Teacher referrals: 4.9%

4. Considerations When Choosing a Job (Multiple Responses)

Wage level: 52.3%, Working hours: 28.1%, Working days/time of day: 24.3%, Work intensity: 23.6%, Job content: 21.1%, Employer attitude: 13.1%, Distance from home/school: 9.9%, Coworkers: 9.3%, Working environment and facilities: 9.1%

5. Industries Worked in Most Frequently (Multiple Responses)

Posting/distributing flyers: 41.6%, Restaurants and dining establishments: 36.1%, Convenience stores: 22.6%, Fast food, bakeries, ice cream shops, cafes: 19.8%, Surveys and research: 18.8%, Store management/sales: 11.4%, Delivery, courier services, and moving: 9.3%

6. Number of Employees at Your Current or Most Recent Workplace

Less than 5 employees: 39.9%, 5-10 employees: 27.2%, Not sure: 17.3%, 10-50 employees: 9.1%, 50+ employees: 6.5%

7. Work Duration and Hours

- Employment Length: Less than 1 month: 32.9%, 1-3 months: 32.9%, 3-6 months: 18.3%, 6 months-1 year: 8.2%, 1+ year: 7.8%
- Days Worked Per Week: 3 days: 27.0%, 2 days: 25.5%, 5 days: 16.3%, 1 day: 13.9%, 4 days: 11.6%, 6 days: 3.0%, 7 days: 2.7%
- Working Hours: Average: 5.2 hours per day (17.5 hours per week)
- Night shifts: 10.8% of respondents (averaging 6.5 hours per week)

8. Compensation

- Payment Structure: Hourly: 44.7%, Monthly: 24.9%, Daily: 13.7%, Weekly: 8.6%
- Average Earnings: Monthly: 833,769.4 won, Weekly: 121,367.1 won, Daily: 62,301.7 won, Hourly: 9,194.4 won

(2020 Minimum Wage Reference: Hourly: 8,590 won, Daily: 66,800 won (8-hour day), Monthly: 1,795,310 won)

9. Workplace Satisfaction Ratings (out of 100)

Coworkers: 69.0, Job Content: 68.9, Hours: 68.1, Pay: 67.3, Work Environment: 65.8, Work Intensity: 62.6

10. Impact of Work Experience (out of 100)

Direct help with living expenses: 64.0, Less time with friends: 47.3, Help with future career planning: 42.0, Lack of sleep: 37.5, Negative feelings about society: 37.2, Interference with studies: 36.6, Mental harm: 34.2, Physical health deterioration: 30.2, Lowered self-esteem: 26.6, Damaged relationships: 22.6

11. Future Work Intentions

Want to continue working: 52.9%, Don't want to work but have no choice: 28.7%, Don't want to work: 18.4%

12. Reasons for Not Wanting to Work (Multiple Responses)

Work was too difficult: 59.3%, Too time-consuming: 41.5%, Not a helpful experience: 41.1%, Underpaid: 23.8%, Impersonal treatment: 16.5%

13. Whether a Labor Contract Was Written

Completed agreement and received copy: 53.0%, Never completed agreement: 28.7%, Completed agreement but received no copy: 18.3%

Article 67 of the Labor Standards Act (Labor Contract): When an employer enters into a labor contract with a person under the age of 18, the employer must specify the working conditions in writing (including electronic documents, as defined in Article 2, Paragraph 1 of the Electronic Documents and Electronic Transactions Act) and provide a copy to the employee.

14. Work Permits and Parental Consent

- Work Permit Status: Started working without permit: 48.4%, Uncertain about permit status: 31.3%, Obtained permit before working: 20.3%

- Parental/Guardian Consent: Provided consent documentation: 72.2%, Did not provide consent documentation: 27.8%

15. Insurance Coverage

Don't know if enrolled in the four major insurances: 41.4%, Not enrolled: 34.8%, Enrolled: 23.8%

Motorcycle Food Delivery in High School

Minjoon obtained his motorcycle license in October 2017, during his freshman year of high school. This qualification opened a new employment opportunity that he pursued throughout high school—delivering for chicken restaurants, Tteokbokki shops, and a motorcycle food delivery service called Burung.

"A motorcycle delivery job pays well, the work isn't difficult, and you get to ride a motorcycle," Minjoon explained.

His introduction to motorcycle delivery came through a friend already working at a local chicken restaurant. The restaurant was owned by a man in his late twenties, with his mother managing the kitchen. The delivery team consisted of three or four drivers, including Minjoon, who at 17 was the youngest, with the oldest being 19. The group included both students and non-students.

Shifts typically ran from 5 PM to 1 AM, or sometimes from 6 PM to 2 AM. With an hourly wage of 10,000 won, Minjoon earned between 2.2 and 2.3 million won a month. When asked about workplace challenges, he replied, "If someone goes AWOL, I have to handle what should be two people's workload by myself. If someone takes vacation, I have to step in as a 'pinch hitter.' I think I worked almost every day without a break."

During the summer vacation of his sophomore year, Minjoon started delivering for a Tteokbokki restaurant in Hongdae, working grueling 12-hour shifts from 5 PM to 5 AM at the same hourly rate of 10,000 won.

For deliveries, Minjoon used the restaurant's motorcycle, during which he experienced two or three traffic accidents. As expected, he covered the cost of vehicle repairs out of his own pocket.

The 2020 Survey on Youth Labor Rights revealed a rise in youth employment in motorcycle delivery jobs, largely driven by the COVID-19 pandemic. The survey raised three main concerns: the high risk of industrial accidents, the negative impact of night shifts on education, and the use of freelance contracting to circumvent labor protections. The survey highlighted that young workers often bear personal responsibility for accidents, rather than recognizing employer liability. Night deliveries, in particular, were noted to disrupt students' academic performance, as these hours are typically meant for studying. Additionally, the fatigue from working late into the night affected their ability to focus in class the following day.

Motorcycles, Money, and Accidents

In addition to restaurant-based delivery work, Minjoon also joined a delivery agency called Burung. He found the opportunity through an advertisement on *Albamon* (a popular job listing platform), visited the local office, and registered as a driver. The onboarding process was straightforward—no resume submission or formal interview was required.

Burung paid 3,000 won per delivery, with additional premiums for nighttime work. After deducting the 500 won per-delivery agency fee,

Minjoon calculated that he needed to complete four to five deliveries per hour to match his 10,000 won hourly wage at the restaurant. By working at maximum capacity, he could potentially earn more than at the chicken restaurant.

"Delivering chicken on a motorcycle is an hourly job," Minjoon explained. "So, when the restaurant is slow, you can still earn money while sitting idle—unlike agency work with Burung, where you can't make money if you're not moving."

With his accumulated earnings, Minjoon purchased his own motorcycle. However, during his senior year of high school, he was involved in a serious traffic accident. The collision left him hospitalized with multiple fractures that required full-body casts. His motorcycle was damaged beyond repair and had to be scrapped.

The accident dampened Minjoon's enthusiasm for motorcycles, and he ultimately decided to quit delivery work altogether.

Straddling Two Worlds: The Struggles of Student Workers

In Korea, part-time work has traditionally been viewed as temporary employment or supplemental income for students, young adults, and housewives. However, recent surveys indicate that a growing number of part-time workers now exceed 40 hours a week, relying on these jobs as their primary source of income. This shift challenges the traditional view of part-time work as a side activity, instead framing it as a form of non-regular employment that includes both short-term and temporary workers.

— Oh Sunjeong (2018), "Concept and Characteristics of Part-Time Labor"

Since starting part-time work in middle school, Minjoon has never received proper documentation of his employment status. His employers never requested parental consent or proof of family relationships, even during his high school years. He never signed a formal labor contract or received wage statements.

As a teenage student, Minjoon regularly worked 12-hour shifts, often until 1 or 2 AM, and occasionally as late as 5 AM. Taking a single day off each week was a challenge, as he was frequently called in to fill in for absent coworkers.

Korean labor law explicitly prohibits minors aged 15-18 from working overtime (beyond five hours per week) or night shifts (unless specially approved by labor commissioners). The law also mandates that all workers, including youth, be granted at least one paid weekly rest day.

However, Minjoon did not receive the legally mandated benefits, such as pay for weekly rest days, night shift premiums (1.5 times the hourly wage), overtime compensation, or holiday pay. Most of his employers operated small businesses with fewer than five employees, exempting them from some premium pay requirements. However, the legal restrictions on night shifts, excessive overtime, and holiday work still applied, regardless of the business's size.

As Kim and Lee (2019) note, Korea's youth policy has historically concentrated on education, overlooking the growing number of working youth. With a focus on high school graduates entering college, the working conditions for young people have been largely ignored, overshadowed by the pressures of college admissions. Nevertheless, public education's core purpose is to prepare students for entry into the labor market as competent individuals. Work experience, especially during youth, plays a crucial role in this transition, and it is essential that the state implement policies that support this vital developmental stage.

After working late into the night for an extended period, Minjoon often overslept and arrived late to school. After classes, he would go straight back to work.

Minjoon, who was both a student and a worker, was denied the protections afforded to either group—neither the support for students nor the legal rights guaranteed to workers.

Between a Part-time Job and a Job

Although Minjoon eventually stopped delivering for a motorcycle food service, his experience with part-time work continued. As a college student in 2020, Minjoon found a job at a bar in Sangsu through Albamon, where he worked for nine months, from March to December.

"The hiring process was always informal," Minjoon explained. "I'd see a job posting, visit the place, express

interest, and they'd ask when I could start. I'd say, 'Tomorrow.' That's how most of my jobs began."

His shifts typically ran from 6 PM to 1 or 2 AM. The bar was managed by a man in his fifties who handled the kitchen. Minjoon's duties included organizing the dining area, distributing menus, taking customer orders, and serving drinks and appetizers. He started with an hourly wage of 9,000 won for the first month, which later increased to 9,500 won.

The work itself was not particularly challenging, and Minjoon found his boss to be kind. However, the COVID-19 pandemic led to frequent restrictions on bar operations. In December 2020, the bar was forced to close due to the ongoing constraints. Minjoon then left and began searching for alternative part-time employment.

Getting a Job at the Hotel

When Minjoon came across a job posting for part-time positions in both the door team and the food and beverage team at Hotel A, he applied for both roles. His interviews were scheduled for the same day, starting with the door team, followed by the food and beverage team two hours later.

Typically, food and beverage interviews were conducted by the general manager, but on this occasion, a concierge from the rooms division stepped in to lead the interview instead. After completing both interviews, Minjoon received job offers from both teams.

Unexpectedly, the concierge who had conducted Minjoon's food and beverage interview presented him with a third option—joining the rooms team instead. Unlike the part-time roles he had originally applied for, the rooms team consisted of interns and full-time employees who interacted directly with guests. This position typically required foreign language proficiency to assist international travelers. Despite Minjoon's lack of English or other language skills, the concierge reassured him that it wouldn't be an issue, possibly influenced by Minjoon's tall stature and friendly demeanor. Minjoon accepted the offer.

He joined the rooms team at Hotel A in December 2020, working there for ten months before leaving just two weeks prior to his military enlistment in October 2021.

Life as a Room Clerk

Minjoon spent his first month at Hotel A undergoing training as a room clerk. His primary responsibilities included staffing the front desk, assisting with luggage for checked-in guests, and escorting them to their rooms. Once in the room, he provided detailed explanations of the room's features and hotel amenities, inquiring if the guests had any additional requests and ensuring their needs were met.

The Hotel A, marketed as a "six-star hotel," featured 250 rooms. On average, the hotel hosted between 190 and 200 guest parties on typical days, and Minjoon personally guided around 20 groups of guests each day.

"When I joined the rooms team, I disclosed my lack of English proficiency, so management made sure I wasn't assigned to foreign guests," Minjoon explained. *"However, hotel policy required all staff to greet guests when making eye contact in hallways or the lobby. If I encountered a foreign guest, I would approach them with 'May I help you?' When they responded in words I couldn't understand, I would say 'Wait a minute' and escort them to a colleague who spoke English."*

Minjoon worked under a three-month labor contract with Hotel A, which was renewable based on performance evaluations. He rotated through four shift patterns: 7 AM to 4 PM, 10 AM to 7 PM, 1 PM to 10 PM, and 2 PM to 11 PM. Work schedules were distributed a month in advance.

His hourly wage was 9,000 won, the minimum wage level. However, Minjoon received a weekly holiday allowance and additional compensation for working on "red days" or overtime—benefits that are legally required. For the first time in his working life, he was enrolled in all four major insurance programs: National Pension, Health Insurance, Employment Insurance, and Workers' Compensation Insurance. After deductions for taxes and these insurance programs, his monthly earnings ranged from 1.6 million to 2 million won.

Stress-Induced Hair Loss

The Hotel A required employees to be fully dressed and prepared for duty 30 minutes before their scheduled shifts. To meet this requirement, Minjoon had to arrive at least one hour before his shift began. For his 7 AM shifts, this meant waking up at 4 AM.

During high school, Minjoon was often late to class, leading many, including myself, to believe he was a "heavy sleeper." However, the reality was that his tardiness was due to working long hours late into the night. To meet his early wake-up time, Minjoon disciplined himself to go to bed early, wake up on his own to his alarm, and prepare for work. My assumption about his struggle with mornings had been completely mistaken.

The rotating four-shift schedule meant his work hours constantly shifted, with holidays (or "red days") requiring overtime. After returning home from work, he was usually exhausted—just enough energy to shower before collapsing into bed. This grueling routine left little room for personal pursuits or relaxation. At only 21 years old, Minjoon began experiencing hair loss, a direct result of work-related stress.

Minjoon's mother (my sister) urged him to quit, insisting it wasn't a "real" job and that he shouldn't have to endure such harsh conditions. Despite this, Minjoon persevered through his first three-month contract, then renewed it for another term, and another after that. He continued working at Hotel A until just two weeks before his military enlistment.

"Everyone here, both the staff and the customers, are all 'silver spoons.'"

The Hotel A offered luxury accommodations with rates reaching tens of millions of won per night. During his time there, Minjoon had the opportunity to see high-profile figures, including the president of a large company and a celebrity. His duties included carrying luggage and retrieving items for guests—predominantly luxury goods. To perform his role effectively, Minjoon had "studied" high-end brands to properly handle guests' designer clothing, bags, and other possessions.

His colleagues predominantly boasted international education credentials. Beyond English proficiency, they typically spoke two or three additional languages, including Japanese, Chinese, Spanish, and Arabic.

A new employee who joined as Minjoon's junior once proudly stated, "I got this job because Hotel A's deputy general manager knows my mother," and claimed that she saved her entire salary while working there. However, it was later revealed that her credit card was actually registered under her mother's account—a "mom card." The luxury items she wore far exceeded what her salary could afford, and could only be explained by her mother's financial support, not her own earnings.

Prospective Career Path

Hotel A offers a structured career progression, starting with a two-year internship that provides the opportunity for advancement into full-time employment. Upon completion of the internship, candidates must pass an examination to transition to permanent employee status. Full-time positions begin with a starting monthly salary of approximately 2.5 million won.

Career progression at Hotel A continues as employees with 7-8 years of service become eligible for management positions. Managers earn around 3 million won monthly, which can total approximately 40 million won annually, including performance incentives. Minjoon's senior colleagues advised him, "Although the salary may not be high, this hotel offers the greatest job security—you don't have to worry about termination."

As Minjoon's mandatory military service date approached, the Hotel began recruiting for intern positions. Management prioritized existing part-time staff for these applications, presenting an opportunity—a rare one, given that no new hires had been made in recent years due to the COVID-19 pandemic. Minjoon, however, felt a deep sense of disappointment at being unable to pursue it because of his impending military enlistment.

Enlisting

"During high school, I was financially irresponsible—spending every won I earned," Minjoon recalled. "But since turning 20, I've worked hard to develop better habits and have

managed to save around 10 million won."

Currently serving his mandatory military duty, Minjoon spends his limited free time studying English. Looking ahead, he has already mapped out his plans for after his discharge: he aims to join a working holiday program, where he can both earn an income and improve his foreign language skills.

Why He Continued Working at Hotel Despite Developing Stress-Induced Hair Loss

Minjoon continued working at Hotel A, even though it made little financial sense. Despite benefits like weekly vacation and overtime pay, the hotel offered the lowest hourly wage of all his jobs. It was more than an hour and a half away from his home, whereas he had previously worked jobs located 20 to 30 minutes from home. Additionally, the hotel required him to arrive at least an hour before his shift started. Given the nature of part-time work, where time directly translates to money, there was no logical reason for Minjoon to continue at Hotel A if his primary goal was to earn more.

The job's toll went beyond logistics, affecting his health and leading to stress-induced hair loss. Despite receiving training for room service, Minjoon struggled as a newcomer, frequently making mistakes that resulted in regular reprimands from senior staff. The hotel's practice of renewing contracts every three months based on performance added additional pressure, as failure could lead to termination. Furthermore, the rigid hierarchy at the hotel intensified the stress, with a junior employee—two years older than Minjoon—being required to address him as "senior" and use honorifics.

Adding to his burden was the expectation to master foreign languages. Minjoon bought

English and Japanese textbooks—subjects he had never studied in school—and used his long commutes to study. His constantly changing four-shift schedule meant his workdays were unpredictable, while mandatory weekend overtime further disrupted any possibility of establishing a routine or achieving balance.

Nevertheless, Minjoon continued working there until just before he enlisted in the army.

Why He Stayed Despite Everything

Even though Minjoon developed stress-induced hair loss during his time at Hotel A, there were several key reasons why he chose to stay.

At his core, Minjoon possessed remarkable sincerity and patience when confronting both physical and emotional challenges. I believe these qualities allowed him to endure difficult working conditions.

Minjoon is also smart, strategically prioritizing future opportunities over immediate financial gain. He understood that the experience he was gaining at Hotel A, particularly in the prestigious "six-star hotel" rooms team, would enhance his future career prospects. Unlike other part-time jobs, the 10 months Minjoon spent in Hotel A's room service department allowed him to accumulate career capital. The hotel even highlighted "career certification" as a key employment benefit when recruiting part-time staff.

"Hotel employees in back-office roles like public relations and marketing typically have higher education, but front-office positions don't necessarily require college degrees. They value language proficiency in English, Japanese, and Chinese. Strong foreign language skills create clear paths to promotion."

Education and Training

Minjoon underwent structured education and training to work with Hotel A's rooms team. His professional development was continuous and well-organized. The first month involved intensive training, followed by ongoing education, evaluations, and skill refinement throughout his tenure.

While demanding, this approach fostered genuine growth. Through this rigorous process, Minjoon gained a comprehensive understanding of hotel room operations, earning not only a formal "certificate of experience" but also valuable real-world expertise.

Structured Career Advancement

Hotel A provided a clear advancement path based on tenure and performance. Minjoon began as a part-time employee, with the potential to progress to intern status (non-regular employment), then to full-time employment, and eventually into supervisory roles.

This structured progression presented a future where improvement was tied directly to personal effort and determination—a system where Minjoon could build something better through his own dedication.

Colleagues and Mentors

Working at Hotel A exposed Minjoon to a new social circle, where he interacted with colleagues fluent in foreign languages and who had lived abroad—experiences far beyond what he had encountered previously.

Throughout our interview, Minjoon often referenced his colleagues and seniors, saying, "Senior A is like this, Senior B approaches things that way, Senior C handles situations differently." These relationships proved invaluable, as his peers and seniors provided him with meaningful insights into potential career paths. Through these workplace mentors, Minjoon first learned about the working holiday program he's now actively planning.

The diverse life experiences of his colleagues became powerful learning opportunities for Minjoon. He observed firsthand how foreign language proficiency could open doors to better positions and promotions, and how working at prestigious establishments like Hotel A—despite modest salaries—could offer long-term stability and future prospects. He witnessed a senior colleague leverage her experience at Hotel A to secure a sales position at a luxury retailer, commanding a significantly higher salary than in her previous role. This kind of career progression has now become a key consideration in Minjoon's own future plans.

More Than a Job

Minjoon majored in tourism at a vocational high school and continued with hotel tourism in college. However, when asked about these choices, his answers lacked conviction—often citing reasons like "other majors are more competitive" or simply "just because." Despite his long history of working in various roles, Minjoon had never truly had the opportunity to reflect on his career aspirations or dreams.

Until now, Minjoon had been focused on the tasks at hand, without giving much thought to his true passions or professional goals. The saying goes, *"You can only dream as much as you know."* His experiences and the world he had been exposed to thus far limited his vision of what could be possible.

It was his experience at Hotel A that finally sparked genuine career interest. There, Minjoon not only performed his duties effectively but also began envisioning a different, more promising future—discovering a profession.

§ *During childhood, we played together often, but once he entered middle school, our interactions dwindled to brief greetings and surface-level exchanges. Meaningful conversations became rare.*

The interview for this project provided a unique opportunity to connect with him as adults. As we spoke at length, I discovered qualities I had never fully appreciated—his remarkable eloquence, genuine warmth, and notably respectful language. Throughout our extensive conversation, not a single profanity escaped his lips. Even when discussing friends he described as "tough," he chose the compassionate framing of "friends who grew up in different environments."

His thoughtful expression reflects something profound: kind words truly do emerge from a beautiful heart.

I thought about the cost of survival along the Eungang River. Not the cost of living—but the cost required simply to survive. My three siblings worked themselves to death in a factory. We were paid far less than the value we created. That year, the official minimum cost of living for a city worker supporting a family of four was 83,880 won. Our mother calculated that the combined income of the three siblings amounted to just 80,231 won. But after deducting insurance premiums, national savings, mutual aid contributions, union dues, welfare costs, and food expenses, only 62,351 won remained. We worked ourselves to death for that money. And our mother lived in constant anxiety.

— Cho Sehee, *The Dwarf Who Shot a Little Ball*

Chapter 5: Jihoon Lee

Around and Around: Back to the Motorcycle Food Delivery Circuit

When I asked Jihoon, my nephew, about his earnings history, he shared that his first significant income—one million won—came from illegal online gambling when he was a first-year middle school student. For him, gambling represented a potential income source rather than mere entertainment. However, this approach ultimately left him burdened with debt. To repay his gambling losses, Jihoon decided to drop out of high school and start working as a motorcycle food delivery driver. Although he has held other jobs—such as frying chicken at a restaurant and managing a café—he consistently returns to motorcycle food delivery, as it offers higher earnings.

Jihoon lacks formal education, specialized skills, or substantial work experience, limiting his earning opportunities to physically demanding jobs with long hours, low pay, or significant risks. This cycle of difficult and hazardous work often results in repeated job losses, pushing him back toward gambling as an alternative source of income. For Jihoon, labor provides neither present stability nor future promise. Work has become disconnected from any sense of hope.

Profile

- Name : Jihoon Lee
- Birth Year : 1999
- Education : High school dropout
- Work Experience : 11 years
- Started Working At : 14 years old
- Occupation History : Reseller, café manager, restaurant staff, office assistant, food delivery driver, etc.

Gambling and Motorcycle Food Delivery

Runaways and Gambling

Jihoon ran away from home for the first time in his first year of middle school—and he needed money. Teaming up with three friends, they each contributed 25,000 won, pooling a total of 100,000 won to place bets on illegal online sports gambling.

The gambling format was simple: participants wagered on match outcomes, predicting winners, losers, or point spreads relative to set thresholds. Each bet cost just 5,000 won, and as long as they had a mobile phone and a bank account, anyone—regardless of age—could participate.

In their first gambling venture, Jihoon and his friends had an improbable stroke of luck, winning 4 million won and splitting it evenly—1 million won each.

"As a middle school freshman, a million won felt enormous," Jihoon recalled. "I wasn't thinking about placing another bet. I was completely focused on what I could buy with this windfall."

According to a 2012 nationwide survey by the Ministry of Gender Equality and Family, 48.3% of the 15,487 middle and high school students surveyed had engaged in online gambling games—including go-stop, poker, and horse racing—at least once in their lifetime as of 2010. The average age of first exposure was 12.4 years, typically during the first year of middle school.

Resellers

In his second year of middle school, Jihoon entered the "reselling" market with 500,000 won—capital acquired through gambling. Reselling involves purchasing sought-after products, particularly limited-edition items, then selling them at markups. While some consumers view rare merchandise as expressions of individuality, others recognize their profit potential. For Jihoon, it was strictly business.

He gathered intelligence on "investment-worthy products" through his local network of friends and older acquaintances. To acquire limited-edition items, he sometimes waited in department store lines for days, while other times, he entered purchase lotteries for highly sought-after products.

The resale market followed unpredictable timelines. Items didn't automatically gain value after purchase—some took weeks or even months to sell at a profit. During these waiting periods, Jihoon stored his inventory at a friend's house. When successful, he could earn up to 100,000 won a week, but timing was crucial. Products initially labeled as "limited editions" could suddenly lose value if companies increased supply, sometimes leaving Jihoon with losses when he failed to anticipate market shifts.

Concerns over transaction security meant most exchanges took place in person to verify authenticity and prevent counterfeit sales.

Jihoon's age often raised suspicions, with one buyer even asking, "How could you afford something so expensive at your age?"

"My limited capital kept me to smaller items like shoes and clothing," Jihoon explained. *"I might sell something worth 500,000 won for 550,000 won. My older connections have larger funds, so they handle higher-value items like designer bags and winter coats, ranging from 1,000,000 to 3,000,000 won."*

By the time he completed middle school, Jihoon had accumulated 3 million won in his bank account.

Debt and Dropping Out of School

Shortly after starting high school, Jihoon ran away from home again. Facing financial pressure, he turned to online illegal gambling, expanding his options beyond sports betting. He accessed platforms offering casino-style games—baccarat, roulette, blackjack, and "all the gambling options available at *Gangwon Land* (the only legal gambling location in Korea for citizens)." These sites had minimal barriers to entry, similar to sports betting: a mobile phone and a bank account were all that was needed, regardless of age. Jihoon gained access to these platforms through his network of friends and older associates.

> *"Many illegal gambling sites exist, but the key factor is their reliability in 'exchanging'—converting digital winnings into actual currency—because some operators simply disappear with users' funds,"* Jihoon explained. *"One major platform has built a reputation for dependable exchanges, likely attracting millions of daily users. You won't find these sites through conventional advertising; word-of-mouth from experienced players is how the knowledge spreads."*

Jihoon exhausted all his reselling earnings and began borrowing from his social circle. This pattern aligns with research from the Korea Criminal Policy Research Institute (2020), which found that adolescents with extended gambling histories often progress from using pocket money to borrowing from peers. Other documented sources of funding include "criminal participation" and "theft from family members."

His debt eventually grew to 5 million won—a substantial amount that forced him to make a life-changing decision. To address the financial burden, Jihoon dropped out of high school and started working as a motorcycle food delivery driver.

The Untold Story of Jihoon's Friends: Gambling in the Streets

Jihoon attended elementary, middle, and high school in Mangwon-dong, starting from kindergarten. Most of his nine friends, now 24, are those he has known since childhood in the neighborhood. Jihoon and his friends share similar life paths—running away from home, turning to gambling, accumulating debt, dropping out of school, and eventually working as motorcycle food delivery drivers.

"Friends fall into four categories," Jihoon explains. "The dedicated ones who go to college, those who finish high school, people like me who fall somewhere in between, and at the bottom, the 'movie thugs'—those involved in criminal activity."

Gambling has been a collective activity for Jihoon and his friends since their first year of middle school. This pattern aligns with findings from the Korea Criminal Policy Research Institute (2020): "80% of online gamblers initiated their gambling because they were 'encouraged by a friend' or 'observed a friend gambling,' while 92% received information about online gambling platforms from friends or older acquaintances." The "2020 Youth Gambling Problem Survey Results," published jointly by the Korea Gambling Industry Integration Supervision Commission and the Korea Gambling Problem Management Center, further notes that "online gambling proliferates through young people's social networks rather than physical environments, making gambling-related harm factors particularly difficult to control."

Some of Jihoon's friends gamble occasionally, others have quit entirely, while some remain deeply entrenched. "Among my nine friends, the average gambling debt is 10 million won. Only one has profited from gambling; the rest of us owe amounts ranging from millions to hundreds of millions of won," Jihoon reveals.

• **Friend 1** carries over 200 million won in gambling debt—60 million in bank loans and 160 million in personal loans from acquaintances. His gambling began in middle school and has continued for over a decade. Although he works as a motorcycle delivery driver, his earnings go toward alcohol rather than debt repayment. Daily drinking has become his way of coping with the overwhelming financial pressure. His parents remain unaware of his gambling and debt. (I also had no idea that Jihoon had gambled and was in debt until I interviewed him. His mother, my sister, still doesn't know.)

"With debts of a few million won, repayment is still possible. But for friends owing 100-200 million won, the situation is hopeless. They receive constant calls from creditors demanding payment, making it hard to maintain mental stability. Many turn to daily drinking, which prevents them from working the next day, creating a vicious, destructive cycle."

• **Friend 2** has accumulated 100 million won in gambling debt. Despite his parents paying off his debts multiple times—leading them to downsize from their home to a small apartment, and eventually to a rental unit—he continued gambling. He entered military service with 100 million won in debt and attempted suicide several times while serving, ultimately receiving a medical discharge. He is currently undergoing treatment for gambling addiction and regularly receives hospital care.

• **Friend 3** is a rare success story. After being discharged from the military, he gambled his 10 million won savings in online illegal gambling and won 400 million won. (I repeatedly questioned the veracity of this claim, but Jihoon insisted it was true.) Immediately after winning, he closed his gambling account to avoid relapse. He invested 150 million won to open a chicken restaurant, bought an Audi for 100 million won, and maintains over 100 million won in cash reserves.

Life as a Motorcycle Delivery Driver

After dropping out of school, 17-year-old Jihoon started working as a motorcycle delivery driver for a chicken restaurant. The restaurant employed two or three other drivers, all between 20 and 24 years old.

The job paid just above minimum wage (5,580 won per hour in 2015), and Jihoon worked "full-time" shifts from noon to 1 AM, totaling 13 hours a day. His monthly earnings ranged from 1.8 to 2 million won. After working for three to four months, he managed to pay off his gambling debts and decided to leave the restaurant.

For the next month or two, Jihoon fell into an aimless routine—sleeping, waking up, playing games, and repeating the cycle. His mother gave him pocket money, but it wasn't enough to live on. Eventually, Jihoon realized he needed to start earning again.

Jihoon then joined "Burung," a motorcycle food delivery service. Becoming a Burung rider was simple: download the app, register, select an office, and choose days off. Working six days a week, Jihoon typically took Mondays off.

The basic delivery fee was 3,200 won, with 100 won going to the office and another 100 won to Burung. The base distance covered was 1.5 kilometers, with an additional 100 won charged for every 100 meters beyond that. Jihoon often expressed frustration that this distance was calculated as a straight line between the starting point and destination, rather than the actual route traveled.

Jihoon aimed to complete at least 70 deliveries a day, occasionally reaching 100. On average, he made seven to eight deliveries per hour, often carrying four to five items in his bag at once. Following all traffic signals would limit him to just three deliveries per hour, so running red lights became routine.

"Accidents happened about once a month," Jihoon explained, "but minor incidents were much more frequent—hitting rear-view mirrors, running into people getting off buses, handlebar collisions, and things like that."

He earned between 200,000 and 250,000 won daily, which translated to 4 to 6 million won monthly. Over two years, he managed to save 40 million won.

"I don't drink or shop much—I consider shopping a luxury. The most expensive thing I own is a 170,000 won hoodie," Jihoon remarked.

The Hidden Costs of Jihoon's Rider Earnings

Jihoon has always had a sharp eye for things, and growing up in Mangwon-dong has given him an intimate knowledge of the area. His previous experience delivering for a chicken restaurant on a motorcycle has also been invaluable. These skills, combined with his environmental knowledge and experience, have made him an asset to Burung's delivery service. Most importantly, Jihoon shows remarkable dedication, working over 10 hours a day, six days a week.

> *"I'm the best at delivering in this neighborhood because I can find almost any location just by looking at the address—no need for navigation," Jihoon proudly claims. "Most people avoid long runs, but I do them, too. A long run usually pays five or six thousand won, and I can pick up several deliveries along the way. Because of this, I've received numerous offers from other offices, like 'We'll lease you a motorcycle for free' or 'We'll cover your insurance.'"*

However, Jihoon's reported earnings as a rider don't account for several significant expenses:

Motorcycle Costs: 200,000 won per month

Jihoon initially bought a second-hand motorcycle for 3 million won and has since purchased five more for various reasons: the desire for a new bike, damage from accidents, the aging of his previous bikes, and the need to restart his delivery career.

Motorcycle Insurance: 200,000 won per month (or up to 1 million won per month)

Jihoon, now 24, started delivering food as a teenager. When he first inquired about motorcycle insurance for delivery services, he was quoted 12.5 million won annually. Industry reports show that insurance premiums for delivery riders in their 20s and 30s typically range from 7 million won to 10 million won per year. To avoid this high cost, Jihoon decided not to purchase the expensive insurance. Instead, he registered his motorcycle and insurance under his mother's name, reducing his premium to around 2 million won per year.

Jihoon uses his own motorcycle for deliveries, but if he were to lease one, daily lease fees would range from 20,000 won to 30,000 won, depending on the motorcycle model, with insurance typically included. For a Yamaha N-Max scooter, the average monthly lease payment would be around 800,000 won.

Fuel Expenses: 400,000 won per month

Jihoon covers approximately 200 kilometers daily on his delivery routes, which results in monthly fuel expenses ranging from 400,000 won to 500,000 won. While the Fuel Price Subsidy System helps offset fuel taxes for buses and trucks, motorcycle delivery workers like Jihoon are not eligible for this benefit.

Accident-Related Costs: 200,000 won+ per month

Jihoon experiences accidents at a rate of about once a month. While some incidents are minor, others have required hospitalization. In each case, Jihoon personally covers the costs for motorcycle repairs, medical bills, and compensation to other parties involved.

"When I was 19, I made an illegal U-turn and collided with a bus. My motorcycle was totaled, and it cost me 1.5 million won to repair. I also had to pay the bus company 3 million won in compensation. My knee still hurts from the injury."

According to Cho Kyujoon (2021), the rising number of motorcycle riders has led to an increase in accidents and injuries. Data from the Korea Expressway Administration shows that in 2019, there were 18,467 motorcycle accidents resulting in 23,584 injuries. This marks a significant rise from 2015, with accidents increasing by 45.9% and injuries by 55.4%. 41% of the accidents involved individuals in their 20s or younger. Additionally, research from Representative Han Jeongae's office (Democratic Party of Korea) found that delivery-related accidents accounted for 45.8% of all industrial accident fatalities among 18-24 year olds between 2016 and June 2019.

Customer Claims and Penalties: 50,000 won per month

Occasionally, Jihoon brings home chicken that a customer rejected due to late delivery. When this happens, he not only loses the delivery fee but also has to cover the cost of the food. Additionally, he frequently incurs traffic violation fines, especially for running red lights during peak delivery hours.

Summary of Costs

Jihoon's minimum monthly fixed costs as a motorcycle delivery rider total at least 1 million won. These costs are already higher than those of a truck courier driver. If Jihoon were to insure his motorcycle under his own name (rather than using family members to lower costs) or lease one, his monthly fixed expenses would range from 1.5 million won to 2 million won. It's important to note that Jihoon's reported income does not include standard employment benefits typically provided in formal jobs, such as vacation pay, overtime compensation, night shift differential, severance pay, and other benefits.

The absence of these benefits, combined with Jihoon's significant expenses, reduces his actual take-home pay, making his seemingly lucrative income far less substantial than it appears.

Twenty Years Old, Old Enough for a "Real Job"

After nearly two years as a motorcycle delivery rider for Burung, Jihoon turned 20. With this milestone came a growing desire for what he considered a "real job."

"When I turned 20, I felt like an adult. When people asked, 'What do you do?' I was embarrassed to say, 'I deliver food.' That's when I realized I needed a real job—whether it was working in a restaurant kitchen or something else."

Despite working as a motorcycle delivery rider for almost three years—paying off debts and even saving money—Jihoon never saw it as a true profession. To him, it was simply a way to make ends meet. A job becomes a job when you can confidently say, "This is what I do."

Café Manager

Motorcycle food delivery was a solitary job, and Jihoon longed for more social interaction. Drawn to the idea of becoming a barista, he enrolled in a training program. Using Albamon, a job site specializing in part-time work, he searched for café manager positions and found one that interested him. He submitted his resume, went through an interview, and got hired.

Having never written a resume before, Jihoon asked me for guidance. I advised him to adapt a template from the internet and draft his own. A few hours later, he sent me his resume and asked if it was acceptable. It contained only three entries: *Education — 1 year of high school (dropped out), Work Experience — 3 years at Burung (motorcycle delivery), Certifications — 2 driver's licenses.*

His résumé, light as a feather, weighed heavy on my heart.

"Later, when I asked the café's general manager why he hired me—a middle school graduate with no

The café operated with 12 full-time employees working in two shifts: an opening shift (9 AM–9 PM) and a closing shift (10 AM–10 PM). The schedule followed a five-day workweek, with seven staff members on duty while five were off. Unlike many cafés that rely on part-time workers, this one allows employees to take qualification tests for promotions to positions like store general manager.

Jihoon's responsibilities included managing the counter, preparing drinks, and baking bread. His pre-tax monthly salary was 2.1 million won—just 100,000 won above the minimum hourly wage—but subject to deductions for four major insurance premiums. In the end, he earned less than half of what he had made as a motorcycle delivery rider.

The café was exceptionally popular, with customers lining up from open to close. During peak summer months, daily sales could reach 10 million won. The job was physically demanding—Jihoon worked 12-hour shifts entirely on his feet. The fast-paced environment and exhausting conditions sometimes led to tension, causing occasional conflicts with customers and even prompting some employees to walk out mid-shift.

After a little over a year, Jihoon resigned from the café. The work was exhausting, but the pay was simply too modest.

Kitchen Support at the Chicken Restaurant

After quitting the café, Jihoon started working at a small chicken restaurant opened by a friend with his parents' support. His role was simple but essential—frying chicken.

The restaurant had just six tables and was run by a small team of three or four friends, including the owner. Rather than handling deliveries themselves, they partnered with a delivery agency. Jihoon worked from 4 PM to 1 AM, earning 2.1 million won before tax. The position included coverage under the four major insurance programs and followed a five-day workweek.

Jihoon's life settled into a cyclical routine: after finishing his shift at 1 AM, he would meet up with friends at a *PC room* (an internet café specialized in gaming), where they played games through the night. He'd sleep through the morning, wake up in the afternoon, and return to work—only to repeat the same pattern after each shift.

This lifestyle continued for about six months, and Jihoon began to question the direction of his life. His income was modest, and he longed for some rest.

Eventually, Jihoon decided to quit the chicken restaurant.

Hospital Office Assistant

Initially, Jihoon sought to return to café work, but the COVID-19 pandemic made finding such positions difficult. After two to three months of searching, a friend connected him with an opportunity as an office assistant at a dental hospital. He worked there for the next six months.

The clinic employed three dentists, four nurses, and three office assistants, including Jihoon. His schedule was a standard five-day workweek, from 9:30 AM to 6:30 PM. The position provided coverage under the four major insurance programs and paid a pre-tax monthly salary of 2.1 million won.

Jihoon's responsibilities included entering incoming medication data into the computer system, organizing supplies in the warehouse, retrieving items requested by nurses, and handling various other errands.

This job introduced Jihoon to numerous workplace norms he had never encountered before. In his previous roles—whether delivering motorcycles, working in cafés, or preparing food at a chicken restaurant—weekends were always peak business times, so having weekends off felt completely new. It was Jihoon's first time signing a salary contract and experiencing the concept of annual leave. This was also his first sedentary job, working at a computer. While he rarely interacted with the doctors, he often shared meals with the nurses and office staff. The social environment was different from anything he had encountered before, as his previous workplaces had been more homogeneous.

The transition felt strange and challenging. Jihoon was working, yet it didn't feel like work. Until then, Jihoon had only known physically demanding jobs, where he was constantly on the move for more than 10 hours a day—especially his motorcycle delivery job, which required constant motion. Sitting at a computer and typing occasionally didn't align with his idea of what work should be.

I reassured him, saying, "This is the perfect job." "Everyone works to make money comfortably like this." "Other people earn money so easily." "If there's downtime, you can shop online or browse the internet." "You'll get used to it in a month or two."

But Jihoon lacked confidence in his abilities. He had never worked with Excel or Word—his computer experience was limited to internet browsing and gaming. The medication names, all in English, posed another challenge. As a result, he often made mistakes and struggled with his tasks. This was a stark contrast to his delivery work, where his skills were highly valued, and multiple offices had even tried to recruit him.

However, over time, Jihoon gradually adapted to both the work itself and the lifestyle it offered.

Facing Prejudice and Losing It All Again

Then, something happened. Jihoon's colleagues at the hospital discovered that he was a "middle school graduate" and had been hired through personal connections. This revelation sparked a strong backlash, particularly from the other office assistants. They had graduated from four-year universities—mostly from the provinces—and had secured their positions through formal hiring processes.

His colleagues, who were four or five years older, began openly mocking him. "You can't work like that because you're only a middle school graduate," they sneered. This was the first time Jihoon had experienced discrimination based on his educational background. When he called me in tears, I told him, "It's something you'll have to face at some point in your life and it may happen again and again."

Jihoon snapped back at his coworkers: "You graduated from universities, and this is all you do?" He later described them as "fat, slow, stuffy people." The situation quickly escalated into workplace conflict.

With little enjoyment in his job, a modest salary, and too much free time, Jihoon turned to gambling—Bitcoin. He had saved 40 million won from his motorcycle delivery days and decided to put it into Bitcoin. It was April 2021—crypto prices were soaring, and Bitcoin dominated news headlines. Unlike his previous experience with online gambling, where friends and older acquaintances had introduced him, Jihoon emphasized that this investment was "on his own initiative."

At first, his investment grew to 50 million won. But within three to four months, market volatility wiped out his entire savings. With no money left, Jihoon quit the hospital and began searching for another job to rebuild his finances. He described this period as *"boring, joyless, and one of the darkest times in my life."*

Around and Around: Back to the Motorcycle Delivery Circuit

Back to the Chicken Restaurant

Jihoon has two friends in the chicken restaurant business. One is the owner of a fried chicken restaurant established by his parents, where Jihoon had previously worked. The other funded his own business with 'profits' from illegal online gambling.

The industry is plagued by harsh working conditions and minimal compensation, making staffing a constant challenge. Ironically, however, the COVID-19 pandemic boosted their delivery sales. Both friends offered Jihoon a job, and he chose the higher-paying position at his gambling-funded friend's restaurant.

Jihoon worked twelve-hour shifts, six days a week, earning between 3.3 and 3.5 million won per month. His friend, now his employer, worked the same grueling hours but took home over 7 million won monthly, pocketing approximately 15 percent of all sales revenue.

After just three months, Jihoon resigned. The physical toll of the job and the complete lack of personal time had become unsustainable.

Back to Motorcycle Delivery

After quitting the chicken restaurant and depleting his savings, Jihoon turned to illegal online gambling. This resulted in a debt of 6 million won.

To pay off his gambling debts, Jihoon reluctantly returned to motorcycle delivery—the very job he had left three years earlier in search of a more stable livelihood. "Riding a motorcycle terrifies me now," he confessed. "But I had no choice. I needed the money."

This time, instead of working for Burung, Jihoon opted for platform-based delivery services like Coupang Eats and Baedal Minjok. His career had come full circle, but with a modern twist: from delivering directly for a restaurant to working through an agency (Burung), and now becoming a "platform worker" in the gig economy.

Burung allowed riders to handle multiple orders at a lower rate per delivery, while Coupang Eats and Baedal Minjok operated on a "one delivery at a time" system, offering higher pay per order. Earnings were comparable—Burung riders could complete seven to eight 3,000-won deliveries per hour, while platform-based workers typically managed three to four 5,000-won deliveries. One key difference is that Burung required more time for order pickups, whereas platform-based services minimized downtime.

The payment structures are also different. Burung provided a virtual account where earnings were deposited and withdrawn as needed. Platform workers, on the other hand, received weekly payouts—earnings from

Wednesday to Tuesday were deposited every Friday at lunchtime.

Previously, Burung's multi-order system incentivized riders to rush, often leading to traffic violations like running red lights. However, with smartphone-based citizen reporting and widespread dash cameras, such violations have become riskier and more costly, reducing earning potential across all services.

Burung operates through regional offices with fixed holidays, while platforms like Coupang Eats and Baedal Minjok offer flexible hours. Platform workers can choose when to rest and when to work, with deliveries available between 9 AM and 2 AM.

As platform work continues to grow, criticism is mounting about inadequate social security measures. The increasing number of motorcycle delivery accidents has prompted the government to mandate industrial accident insurance enrollment, though implementation remains problematic.

"If a delivery worker earns more than 800,000 won per month on a single platform, the industrial accident insurance fee is waived," Jihoon explained. *"However, I've never met anyone who has received compensation for an industrial accident while working as a motorcycle delivery rider."*

Before Enlistment

It's been six months since Jihoon returned to motorcycle delivery. Unlike his previous approach, he no longer pushes himself to the limit. Working for Coupang Eats and Ethnic Delivery, he earns a base rate of 4,200 won per delivery, with higher rates during peak hours—the lunch rush (11 a.m. to 1 p.m.) and dinner rush (6 p.m. to 8 p.m.). By strategically scheduling his shifts, Jihoon can make around 100,000 won in just five to six hours of work each day.

"There's nothing difficult about my job now, except standing for long periods."

Jihoon's immediate future involves mandatory military service. As a middle school graduate, he is eligible for Social Service Worker rather than standard military duty.

Now his primary goal is to use his delivery earnings to pay off his gambling debts before enlistment. If he manages to clear his debts ahead of schedule, Jihoon hopes to spend a month working at a guesthouse in Jeju Island before starting his service obligation.

Can Jihoon Escape the Cycle of Motorcycle Delivery?

Jihoon's gambling habit began in middle school, initially as what he saw as a way to "make money." While not a constant activity, he turned to gambling whenever financial struggles arose—whether it was running away from home or facing unemployment.

According to *Developing a Manual for Intervention of Online Gambling Problems among Adolescents* (2020), published by the Korea Youth Counseling and Welfare Development Institute, several risk factors make gambling addiction particularly difficult to overcome: ▸ Viewing gambling primarily as a source of income, ▸ Holding irrational beliefs about winning, ▸ Being influenced by social circles that reinforce gambling through their perceived successes. Jihoon, unfortunately, embodies all these risk factors, making his situation especially difficult to escape.

The cycle is vicious. Gambling leads to debt, and debt inevitably drives him back to motorcycle delivery. Despite the physical risks of the job, he continues to return to it because, in his view, it remains the only viable way to earn what he considers "substantial" income. To this day, he remains trapped in this unbroken cycle, still working as a motorcycle delivery rider to pay off his gambling debt.

Jihoon has made several attempts to leave motorcycle delivery behind. He worked as a café manager for a year, fried chicken at a restaurant, and even took on a role as an office assistant at a hospital—despite the challenges of having only a middle school education. However, every job came with its own set of hardships, differing only in degree and nature.

Financially, the pay was barely above minimum wage. In the café, he earned just 2 million won for 12-hour shifts. At the chicken restaurant, he could make 2 million per month working eight-hour days, five days a week, or 3.3 million won if he worked 12-hour shifts, six days a week. Regardless of the job, his earnings were determined primarily by the number of hours worked, with little opportunity for skill development or career advancement.

As Youngmin Shin et al. (2016) noted in "A Study on Stratification of Working Hours in

Korea": "Social polarization and stratification are reflected in working hours, and deepening stratification can also lead to stratification of working hours. Working hours depend on the quality of jobs that individuals can obtain, and the quality of these jobs is determined by the level of human capital that individuals have access to."

Jihoon's limited formal education, lack of specialized skills, and minimal relevant work experience have significantly narrowed his options for earning a "substantial" income. As a result, he is largely confined to physically demanding jobs or grueling work that requires excessively long hours.

The combination of long hours, physically demanding work, and inadequate compensation creates an unsustainable employment pattern. Research by Yoon et al. (2007) confirms that low-wage workers tend to have significantly shorter job tenures compared to their higher-paid counterparts. Workers who start in low-wage positions face greater challenges during job transitions and struggle to maintain stable employment.

Working dangerous, hard, and long hours, Jihoon repeatedly quits his jobs.

Even with a decade of dedicated service in motorcycle delivery, restaurant work, or café management, Jihoon's advancement opportunities remain virtually nonexistent. Neither promotion pathways nor skills development leading to technical positions appear accessible. His earnings remain anchored to minimum wage regardless of tenure, while the physical risks of his work actually increase over time. Meanwhile, none of these positions offer meaningful job security or long-term stability.

¶ *Jihoon currently earns enough to support himself, but his income offers no room for savings or financial security. This precarious situation leaves him vulnerable to unexpected events such as illness, injury, job loss, or family responsibilities.*

If Jihoon were to marry someone with a similar earning capacity (2 million won each, totaling 4 million won), they might manage temporarily. However, if they had a child and one parent needed to stay home, their household income would drop to 2 million won—insufficient to support a family of three without significant hardship.

Furthermore, Jihoon has no safeguards like pensions, insurance, or severance pay.

§ Before interviewing Jihoon, I prepared myself mentally, wondering how open he would be during our conversations.

Just as this book began with my Dad's story, it fittingly concludes with Jihoon's. Despite the 50-year gap between their experiences, striking parallels emerge: a challenging family environment, starting work at a young age, and enduring hard labor. However, there is a significant difference between them. My Dad held onto the belief that hard work would eventually lead to improvement. For Jihoon, though, work offers no such promises. It provides neither present stability nor future happiness. In his experience, labor fails to generate wealth, improve living conditions, or provide security.

Eunjin Kang: Me

- Born in 1981

I have 15 years of professional experience, having worked as a journalist, performance marketer, and PR manager in media organizations, gaming companies, and tech firms.

I graduated from a foreign language high school and pursued both undergraduate and graduate studies. I am fluent in English and Spanish and hold certifications in marketing and computer skills. Through managing multi-billion-dollar marketing budgets and leading global PR and marketing initiatives, I have consistently advanced in my career and seen salary growth with each job transition. Above all, I consider myself fortunate.

School Days

I was in my third year of middle school when my Dad declared bankruptcy in 1996. If the bankruptcy had occurred when I was in elementary school, unaware of the importance of studying, or during high school when I would have been facing college entrance exams like Jiyoung, my situation could have been much harder.

Although I didn't attend a private educational institute or receive tutoring, my teachers provided me with workbooks and supported me in earning a scholarship. Thanks to the unwavering help from my family, teachers, and others, I was able to gain admission to a four-year university in Seoul.

Part-time Job vs Scholarship

During my freshman year of college, I secured a part-time job at a pizzeria. My Dad, who ran a motorcycle courier, advised against working while studying, suggesting that there would be plenty of employment opportunities after graduation. He also pointed out that I would earn more through scholarships than I would by working part-time. His financial calculations turned out to be accurate.

A part-time job, working four hours a day while attending classes, typically generates about 200,000 won a month. Even with full-time work on weekends, I was only making around 100,000 won more. However, considering the cost of tuition—2,000,000 won per semester—a scholarship proved to be far more beneficial. After realizing this, I decided to quit my job to focus on my studies, which allowed me to earn a scholarship.

I relied on financial support from my parents for essential expenses, including meals and transportation. For additional costs such as textbooks, academic fees, and extracurricular activities, I worked part-time as a tutor. This job didn't interfere with my study time.

Upon completing my degree, I faced challenges securing employment. During this time, my Mom, who worked in janitorial services, suffered a brain hemorrhage and required hospitalization. I initially took on the responsibility of caring for her, but soon after, my Dad quit his motorcycle delivery job to take over her care. With this, I was able to resume my job search and eventually found employment.

Professional Journey

Throughout my career, I've worked predominantly for small and medium-sized enterprises with fewer than 300 employees. Despite their size, these companies offered stable employment with full-time status and benefits.

Throughout my tenure, I experienced consistent salary increases and timely promotions. The organizations provided comprehensive employee benefits, including professional development opportunities, educational reimbursement, flexible work arrangements, sabbatical leave, and enhanced healthcare services.

I advanced my career by transitioning between companies approximately every three years. Each move resulted in salary increases and equity compensation through stock options. As a result, my current salary is now three times what I earned when I first started.

Journalism

In 2004, I entered South Korea's rapidly changing digital media landscape. Paran, then a leading portal site, strategically secured exclusive content agreements with five major sports publications, creating an immediate content vacuum for competing portals like Naver and Daum. This presented a significant opportunity for emerging internet-based news organizations, increasing the demand for new journalistic talent.

For recent graduates like myself, this was an unprecedented opening. The traditional barriers to entering journalism—once formidable and tightly controlled—suddenly became more accessible. Journalism, a respected profession across various sectors, became a viable path for me.

IT industry

In 2010, I joined the public relations department of a software company at a pivotal moment in technology—the launch of Apple's groundbreaking iPad. The company developed iPad applications as part of a new business initiative, and I had the opportunity to contribute as a planner. This experience broadened my perspective on technology and inspired me to pursue graduate studies in digital media and the IT industry.

After completing my advanced degree, I transitioned into performance marketing, an emerging field with potential, joining an international gaming company. Despite having no prior experience in performance marketing, I was able to step into the role due to the growing demand and limited expertise in the area at the time. The global reach of the IT sector offered unique opportunities, and I had the privilege of managing multi-billion-dollar marketing and advertising budgets targeting international markets in the United States, Europe, and Asia. This experience of overseeing substantial budgets for a global audience became a key asset in my professional development.

Start-up

In 2017, I joined an innovative artificial intelligence startup, a role that perfectly aligned with my accumulated expertise—international market insights, strategic marketing acumen, and public relations skills. The company thrived due to its innovative AI technology and a team of exceptionally talented professionals. The startup experienced significant growth, expanding both domestically and internationally. This journey culminated in 2021 with a successful exit, bringing tangible financial rewards to every team member.

I consider myself fortunate.

§ *Some achievements can be attributed to fortunate circumstances, while others result from personal capability. When favorable opportunities seem to repeatedly arise for one person, it's not merely luck—it reflects a structure where opportunities are created, often not equally available to everyone.*

Epilogue

The Working Poor represent a fundamental contradiction in our economic system—individuals who remain trapped in poverty despite their hard work. My family falls into this category.

This label carries a dual meaning: Hierarchy and Class. The term "working" places us within the laboring class—those who sell their labor for wages. Meanwhile, "poor" situates us within the economic class of poverty, lacking the resources necessary to maintain a basic standard of living by societal standards.

Thus, our family's identity is shaped by two key factors: our place in the labor hierarchy and our economic status as the impoverished.

When poverty endures despite diligent labor, it erodes the very foundation of worker pride. The implicit social contract—that honest work should meet one's needs—becomes broken, leaving not only financial hardship but also a deep sense of betrayal.

Poverty

"For a long time, poverty has been a major concern for scholars and policymakers. This means that poverty is not only an individual problem, but also a social problem." — Sungju Yoon (2018)

I set out to document my family's labor history—a narrative of hard work, effort, and perseverance. Yet, as the story unfolded, another one emerged beneath the surface: the unrelenting shadow of poverty that has trailed us despite our tireless labor.

Each time a social crisis hit—whether the IMF crisis or COVID-19—our economic vulnerability grew even more pronounced. When family responsibilities expanded to include supporting children, parents, or siblings, or as illness struck or job loss occurred, the entire household felt the financial strain. And poverty is expensive: rising rent, mounting medical bills, and accumulating interest payments.

In response, we worked longer hours, accepted more physically demanding jobs, and undertook increasingly dangerous work. Yet the compensation for this escalating sacrifice barely sustained us at subsistence level. This paradox haunts me: If we work with such intensity and dedication, why does poverty persist? What does it mean when labor—supposedly the pathway to economic mobility—fails to lift one out of hardship?

The answer lies not in individual shortcomings but in structural realities. The poverty experienced by the working poor is not a personal failure but a predictable outcome of systems designed to extract maximum labor while providing minimum compensation. My family's story is not one of insufficient effort but of encountering barriers that no amount of individual industriousness can overcome alone.

Inheritance

"The working poor enter the labor market early, often from poor families, but are characterized by low-wage, low-skilled, and precarious employment from the outset, and are trapped in a cycle of employment and unemployment as they move through peripheral labor markets." — Geumsil Na (2005)

I deliberately tried not to address the issue of succession in my family's story. There is something deeply unsettling about acknowledging the persistence of economic inheritance in a society that prides itself on meritocracy.

We no longer live in a formal caste system where status is explicitly assigned at birth, where marriage is restricted to one's social class, or where career paths are determined by family lineage. Yet beneath the surface of mobility, the mechanisms of inheritance continue to function with precision. The educational attainment of parents, their income levels, and their occupational status serve as powerful predictors of their children's future education, earnings, and career paths.

The data is clear: children born into poverty are disproportionately likely to inherit it. This inheritance isn't passed down through legal documents or ceremonial rituals but through the accumulated disadvantages of limited opportunities, scarce resources, and constrained prospects.

This reality stands in stark contrast to the society we should strive for—a society where every individual has meaningful access to quality education and dignified employment, regardless of their parents' educational background, job status, or income level. The fundamental principle must be that any form of honest labor, in any sector, deserves compensation that upholds human dignity.

The inheritance of economic status is not inevitable—it is shaped by policy choices, resource distribution, and the values we uphold as a society.

Beyond Minimum Wage

"May I ask how much you make?" This question was always difficult for me, pushed to the back of my mind because my mouth wouldn't form the words. The blood, sweat, and tears of a laborer—and how much they are paid for it—are intimate and private matters. — Nam Bora et al., Hell of Intermediate Exploitation

While writing, one of the most frequently searched pieces of information was the minimum hourly wage each year. The minimum wage became a benchmark for my family, determining whether we were getting by or struggling. For many workers—not just my family—survival hinges on the minimum wage, and for them, a "better job" often simply means earning a bit more than that baseline.

The minimum wage isn't just a starting point for temporary or part-time positions; it serves as the foundation for all low-wage jobs. It's not only about making a living; it's about safeguarding the fundamental dignity of workers.

Who has the power to set these wages, and what principles guide their decisions? Consider CEOs who earn hundreds of times more than their average employees. Does their contribution truly warrant such vast disparities?

My sister Yoojung's experience illustrates this reality. She earned only minimum wage at her part-time jobs, but when she found work as a truck courier, she finally made enough to support her family of three.

This reveals a crucial truth: our salaries are determined not by our individual abilities or performance, but by the social and economic structures our society has created and maintains.

Occupation

The poverty and employment insecurity experienced by youth demands our attention because its effects reverberate throughout their entire lives. Early decisions about marriage, childbearing, education, and training significantly determine one's labor market participation and lifetime earnings well into middle and old age. — Ahn JuYeop and Hong SeoYeon (2002)

Occupation represents more than mere survival. A job should be something one pursues for a period of time, aligned with personal interests and abilities, providing not just financial security but also social connection and a sense of fulfillment.

Yet this ideal remains distant for many. Consider Minjoon, who has worked continuously since his third year of middle school—six years of uninterrupted labor. But his work wasn't a "job"; it was only a series of part-time positions. Or Jihoon, delivering food on his motorcycle for over three years, earning just enough to gradually pay down his debts while still searching for a "real job."

I found myself unable to ask Minjoon and Jihoon about their dreams. In today's reality, the concept of a dream has been reduced to the pursuit of stable employment. For many young people, simply having a job has become the ultimate aspiration.

Platform Labor in the Digital Age

For decades, labor was synonymous with employment. Our regulatory frameworks and social protections were built upon this fundamental equation. Yet as observed, this "labor=employment" equation has fractured in

Traditional low-wage occupations are increasingly being absorbed into the platform economy. Cleaning workers, transportation workers, and many others have been transformed into "platform workers"—technically independent contractors, practically dependent laborers.

This transformation has elevated the status of consumers, who now enjoy unprecedented access to services—easier, faster, and cheaper than ever before. The labor of low-wage workers has become increasingly accessible at the tap of a screen.

But this convenience comes at a profound cost. Workers' rights have steadily eroded as labor is devalued, subjected to relentless competition, and fragmented into discrete tasks. Companies hide behind "algorithms" that determine pay rates and work distribution, removing human accountability from the equation.

This reality reveals an uncomfortable truth: when your rights as a worker are weakened, your ability to exercise your rights as a consumer is ultimately compromised as well. The degradation of labor protections creates a system that eventually undermines everyone's economic security and dignity.

The Dignity of Labor

The working poor—comprising 60% of those in poverty in our society—face a triple threat: low wages, informal employment arrangements, and the constant risk of restructuring in microenterprises. This precarity has only intensified in the wake of global financial crises, with the heaviest burdens falling on the most vulnerable: micro-entrepreneurs, day laborers, young people entering the workforce, and women returning after career breaks. — Byunghee Lee and colleagues (2010)

I resist the notion of viewing the solution as freeing workers from labor itself. The true "happy ending" lies not in freedom from work, but in ensuring that labor's intrinsic value is properly recognized—creating conditions where workers can perform their duties safely, with dignity, and even with a sense of fulfillment.

Workers are not objects deserving pity or sympathy. They are individuals who approach their labor with pride and inherent dignity. As such, they deserve to be treated with genuine respect and appreciation for their contributions to society.

This perspective reveals a fundamental truth: labor represents both a human duty and a human right.

References

Ahn, J. Y., & Hong, S. Y. (2002). Socioeconomic characteristics of the poor and poverty transition: Focusing on the post-crisis period. *Korean Journal of Social Work*.

Byun, G. (2012). A study on the factors of working poverty among young adults: Focusing on the effects of employment insecurity and employment status on poverty transition. *Korean Journal of Social Work*.

Cho, K. J. (2021). Features and problems of delivery platform labor. Korea Labor Institute.

Han, Y. (2010). Estimating the elasticity of academic achievement levels using educational production functions. *Curriculum Evaluation Research*.

Han, Y. (2017). Long-term effects of youth job characteristics and implications for youth employment measures. Korea Development Institute.

Hwang, K. (2021). Analysis of the time it takes for young people to get their first job. Korea Employment Information Center.

Jang, J. Y. (2020). The scale and characteristics of platform workers. Korea Labor Institute.

Kim, H. W. (2009). Analysis of the characteristics and economic activities of female household heads - Focusing on comparisons with female spouses. Korea Labor Institute.

Kim, K. H. (2009). Differences in the influence of income class on academic achievement. Korea Life Sciences Association.

Kim, S. J., Lee, J., & Lee, S. (2018). Changes in economic activity and economic status of households due to illness and policy issues. Korea Institute of Health and Social Affairs.

Kim, S. S., Kim, J. H., & Kim, Y. S. (2007). Factors affecting changes in adolescents' academic achievement: Applying the latent growth model. *Korean Youth Studies*.

Koo, S. (2017). A phenomenological study on the growth experience of part-time youth. *Journal of the Korean Content Association*.

Lee, B. H. (2008). A study on the influencing factors of wage determination. *Proceedings of the 9th Korea Labor Panel Conference*.

Lee, B. H., Kim, Y. S., & Park, J. S. (2010). The working poor in Korea: Current status and policy implications. Korea Labor Institute.

Lee, J. R. (2010). The effects of family resources on adolescents' academic achievement: Examining the mediating effects of parenting attitudes and private education. Korean Society for Child Study.

Lee, J. Y. (2017). The effect of children's educational attainment on income class transfers between parents. Korea Institute of Labor Economics.

Lee, K. H., & Min, I. (2016). A study on intergenerational transfers of occupational and income classes. Korea Labor Institute.

Lee, S. R., Kim, H. J., & Lee, Y. S. (2012). A policy study to improve the employment problem of young adults with less than a high school education. Korea Labor Institute.

Lee, Y. (2015). The effects of parenting behavior on adolescents' career maturity: The mediating effect of peer relationships. Korean Society of Family and Education.

Lee, Y. K. (2018). Analyzing changes in young adults' subjective class consciousness and influencing factors on the possibility of class mobility. *Korean Social Research*.

Lim, S. H. (2006). Determinants of poverty exit: Focusing on economic activity characteristics. *Social Security Research*.

Moon, H. J., Kim, S. Y., & Choi, J. Y. (2015). A study on the changing role of family income in college enrollment. Korea Labor Institute.

Na, G. (2005). A study of the determinants of poverty exit among the working poor: Focusing on the pathway constraints in the labor market of the working poor. *Korean Journal of Social Welfare.*

Nam, B., Kim, J., & Lee, H. (2019). The Hell of Middle-Class Exploitation. Seoul: Hankyoreh Publishing.

Nam, Y. N. (2009). The polarization of classes and changes in daily life and consumption after the foreign exchange crisis. Korean Society for Survey Research.

Oh, S. (2018). Concept and characteristics of part-time work. Korea Labor Institute.

Park, C., Lee, J., & Kim, S. (2013). The emotional labor status of product salespersons and telephone counselors. Korea Labor Institute.

Park, J. A., Kim, H. S., & Lee, S. J. (2017). Poverty and labor experiences of non-college-going youth: Focusing on general high school graduates. *Lifelong Learning Society.*

Park, J. K. (2003). Poverty of female heads of households and socioeconomic characteristics of poor households. Korean Society of Health and Social Affairs.

Park, S. (2020). Analyzing the determinants of time poverty by income class. *Health and Social Research.*

Park, S. (2021). A study on the actual situation of youth labor and labor rights awareness. Kyungdong University.

Shin, H. M., & Oh, E. J. (2014). The current status and policy issues of career and employment of high school graduates. Korea Women's Policy Research Institute.

Shin, Y., & Hwang, K. (2016). A study on the stratification of working hours in Korea. *Korea Social Policy.*

Sung, E., & Won, J. (2014). Analysis and implications of poverty exit factors for poor households: Focusing on employment activation of the poor. Korea Economic Institute.

Tak, G. (2004). A study on the improvement of the commercial paper system and the role of credit insurance system. Yonsei University.

Yoon, S. J. (2018). Analysis of the relationship between poverty status and labor mobility of the working poor. Korea Employment Information Institute.

Yoon, Y. K., Lee, J. H., & Park, S. Y. (2007). Current status of labor market polarization and countermeasures: Focusing on the effect of industrial structure change. Korea Institute of Health and Social Affairs.

Korea Labor Institute. (2001). A study on labor market instability before and after the foreign exchange crisis. *Journal of Korean Labor Economics.*

Korea Labor Institute. (2004). Changes in the wage gap between educational levels and factor analysis.

Korea Labor Institute. (2005). The impact of family background on academic achievement: Gender differences.

Korea Labor Institute. (2007). A study of the determinants of poverty exit among the working poor: Focusing on the pathway constraints in the labor market of the working poor. *Korean Journal of Social Work.*

Korea Labor Institute. (2012). Changes in the educational attainment gap between classes: Focusing on the effects of school policies. *Sociological Studies in Education.*

Korea Labor Institute. (2020). Pathways to problem gambling among adolescents: Application of the problem and pathological gambling pathway model. *Health and Social Research.*

Korea Women's Development Institute. (1998). Status of women's vocational training and development of promising occupations.

Korea Youth Counseling and Welfare Development Institute. (2020). Developing a manual for intervention of online gambling problems among youth. Ministry of Gender Equality and Family Affairs.

National Human Rights Commission. (2004). A study of the poor from the perspective of 'social exclusion'.

National Human Rights Commission. (2019). Survey on the human rights situation of platform labor workers.

National Human Rights Commission. (2020). Survey on the situation of youth labor rights.

Title: The Hustle : A Korean Family's Escape from the Margin

Author: KANG EUNJIN

Publisher: Fly the Nest Books

© 2025 Fly the Nest Books

All rights reserved. No part of this publication may be reproduced, distributed, or transmitted in any

www.ingramcontent.com/pod-product-compliance
Lightning Source LLC
Chambersburg PA
CBHW051550250726

48653CB00004BA/1074